A
SMALL
FARM
IN
MAINE

A SMALL FARM IN MAINE

TERRY SILBER

Illustrations by Glenna Lang

A Richard Todd Book

HOUGHTON MIFFLIN COMPANY / BOSTON

1988

Library of Congress Cataloging-in-Publication Data
Silber, Terry, date.
A small farm in Maine / Terry Silber.
p.   cm.
"A Richard Todd book."
Bibliography: p.
ISBN 0-395-37911-3
1. Farm life — Maine. I. Title.
S521.5.M2S55   1988   87-29040
630'.9741 — dc 19   CIP

Printed in the United States of America

S 10 9 8 7 6 5 4 3 2 1

To Mark and Jacob

CONTENTS

A
SMALL
FARM
IN
MAINE

INTRODUCTION

WE CAN neither see nor hear any of our neighbors. The last stretch of road to the farmhouse is dirt, and it ends about a hundred feet from the kitchen door. If we want to shop for food, we need to travel about twenty miles, and if we want to purchase supplies for our farm, we need to go at least that far, if not fifty miles farther. During the summer months, I see more hawks flying over our fields than I do planes. Our mailing address is a rural free delivery number, and the postman negotiates his route in a four-wheel-drive vehicle. We pump our own water from a well that was dug down some twenty-five feet and carefully lined with field stones, probably by the Ellises in the early part of the last century. When we lose our electricity, which we do whenever there are heavy winds, rains, or snow, we heat and cook on the kitchen woodstove and light our house with kerosene lamps.

The floors of the farmhouse are old, wide spruce boards that we have sanded free of their gray paint. Unfortunately, the roof is still original, and it sags a bit more each year, so one summer very soon we will have to tear it off and completely replace it. We have yet to insulate and plaster the ceiling of our attic bedroom, so I look up each night at the hand-hewn beams and the roof boards, which bear the marks of cross-cut saws. I will be somewhat sorry when we do finish off that room, because it is there that I can most clearly re-create a sense of the effort that went into building this house.

When the moon is full and the ground is covered with snow,

there is enough natural light outside to see the color of the mittens and jacket that I've put on to walk to the barn. On a cloudy night when the trees are fully leafed out, the farmhouse and grounds are totally and wonderfully dark. It is the kind of darkness that seems to expand the distance between us and the rest of the world. It is a darkness that can make me feel, for a brief moment, altogether separate.

The other evening, shortly after dinner, a cow moose and her calf ambled across our back lawn, stopping for a moment to graze and exchange glances with our two horses in the pasture before sauntering off through the pines. We could hear branches snapping beneath their hooves until they were well off into the woods.

Loons come every spring to nest on North Pond, about a mile from our land; we hear them clearly morning and evening. The whippoorwill hasn't arrived yet this summer. I notice its call only at night, when its distinctive melody is woven among the flutelike notes of the hermit thrush.

It is time to mow the winter rye that we planted as a cover crop on parts of the upper fields. That means we will have to wrestle the mowing attachment onto our old tractor, a job that none of us enjoys. But if we don't get it done soon, we will not be able to turn the horses out to graze, and it is getting much too late in the season to be buying feed hay. We also have to finish liming and seeding the uppermost field, so we can reclaim that area for haying and grazing as well. Whatever the season, I am fully aware of the tasks that must be done, and I am working to fit those in with the tasks that ought to be done and those that we would like to include if we could find the time. Before us, the Ellises, Coles, Sullivans, Waterhouses, Turners, Dunns, and Trasks must have been kept just as busy by this place.

I never expected to end up on a farm in Maine, least of all one that is located no more than twenty miles from the small mill town in which I was born. Since I left to go to college, I have lived in five states, two countries, and more than two dozen apartments or houses. Since graduation, I've worked in eight institutions, each of them rather interesting, some challenging, and some that are considered prestigious. At thirty, I was setting my course toward professional accomplishment of a rather traditional sort. Now my work exists far outside the boundaries of well-known institutions. I make a living off the land in a way that is not explainable with any label that can be easily understood, much less counted on to garner status. I live on a real family income that places me close to the national poverty level. What's more, I grow more and more certain that I will live out the rest of my life here, although I am not certain whether I should be scornful of my contentment or grateful for my discovery.

I am one of thousands of men and women who moved back to the land. We homesteaders, the urban dropouts of the sixties and seventies, made it fashionable to come to the country. In fact, we developed homesteading into yet another national industry. Magazines, tools, machinery, cooperatives, political movements, clothing, and architectural styles were first produced by and for the homesteaders, and then refined for the weekend dropouts. The movement produced millions of active and sympathetic followers as well as a number of prominent spokesmen. The men and women who became regionally and nationally visible did so principally because of their political and social organizing, but also because of their increased awareness of and appreciation for homesteading skills and crafts. The movement also gave rise to a number of proselytizers and backwoods philosophers — earnest ones, simplistic ones, committed ones, and opportunistic ones.

We will probably not be able to evaluate the impact that this small movement had and will have on attitudes in this country in the immediate future, since we are still too close to it to sort out the faddish responses from the long-term social impact. We do know, however, that the rush to settle in a cabin in the country has peaked and all but disappeared. We also know that a goodly number of us who participated in the movement became disappointed and disillusioned by its realities. Cities and suburbs are now filled with people who have dropped back in and returned to graduate schools, professional careers, and traditional upwardly mobile aspirations.

Making a living and a satisfactory life for yourself is not easy in the country, and I think that the back-to-the-land movement was destined to end, primarily because many of its proponents confused the choices they were making. It might be possible to disengage from the demands of urban and professional institutions, but nowhere can one disengage from the basic needs for food, shelter, and at least a modest coordination of one's life with a community of people. The rural communities that we homesteaders moved into were less populated, less affluent, less cosmopolitan than the cities we left behind. They were no more provincial, only provincial in different ways. The rural people we all came to know were as noble, intelligent, ignominious, and ignorant as the people we knew and didn't get to know in the cities. We brought ourselves to the country and tried to imagine that we had come to a place that was saner, less troubled and demanding. But we still had to attend to our own growth and needs in places that were without the benefits of urban stimulation.

As each of us picked our way through a series of experiences, we fared more or less well according to our individual needs for the rewards that are intrinsic in rural life. There were so many young men and women who were convinced that they were the first generation truly to experience the wonder of childbirth, the pleasure of baking their own bread, the virtue of not eating meat. And after we had all found our beautiful retreats, had our babies, fed ourselves well, and learned to make baskets and build shelters, we were forced to get on with the other necessities of life, not the least of which was to make a living from year to year, raise our children, and continue to educate and nourish ourselves.

I believe that rural life has to be viewed as an aesthetic choice, not an ethical one. Lives can be as well-intentioned in corporate

America as on the farm. There was a lot about the spirit of the back-to-land movement that was indulgent, naive, and self-righteous. Participants often spoke of their choices as though they were moral rather than personal. But sooner or later most of us realized that we had given up enormous rewards from participation in urban work and cultural life that are not easy to replace with real satisfaction in a rural environment.

Rural life can sustain people if the things that most interest those people are rural by their very nature. In many cases, we back-to-the-land participants did not have it in mind to make our living off the land, and yet the mythology of rural life that attracted us was based not only on the beauty of a physical environment but on an old model of agrarian communities that were in fact unified by the commonality of work and by shared interests and goals.

Small-scale agrarian communities have been on the decline in New England for more than half a century. Like many of the inhabitants of such communities before us, a goodly percentage of homesteaders were forced to seek employment away from the farm. When we did, we began to commute away from our retreats and rejoin the work forces of towns and cities at some distance from our land. The need to make a living led to changes in our attitudes and conflicts between our original and emerging goals. When the romance of settling on the land wore off and we reentered the more common workplaces around us, we often began to search again for the familiar rewards and amenities of the suburban and urban lives we had recently abandoned.

There have been numerous times during the past decade when I've thought about how different my life would be now if I had continued with my urban career. I've reflected most seriously when I've felt discouraged with our efforts to make a living off our farm. I've reflected most honestly when trying to find the words to make my son understand why we are here.

It would be easy to say that this spot is so extraordinarily beautiful that no one needs an explanation for being here. But I can remember looking at this homestead for the very first time. It was and is a modest place. The farmhouse is classically simple. The land around it is a common mixture of fields and rolling hills. There are no great views, and the river that marks one of our boundaries is shallow and rocky. This farm has, however, sheltered and provided for eight different families. The land has been worked for one hundred and fifty years. This homestead is one of thousands that has played a particular role in the history of rural New England. The longer that I live in this farmhouse, the more I work to restore the land, the stronger becomes my bond to the place and to its history. My familiarity with this place continually feeds my sense of its beauty.

I think that in the end, we do — if we are willing to take the risks — make choices that will let us live out our lives in an environment that will most nurture our needs. The communities that we choose to live in must ultimately help us support our individual senses of ourselves. The work that we choose to sustain ourselves and our families has to have some meaning and the appropriate rewards if we are simply to get out of bed each day and put in all the effort.

I've been acquainted with my land now for more than twenty years, and I have had the great good fortune to discover reasons for staying. No other place in my life has exacted so much from me, in terms of either physical or intellectual effort. No place has held out such rewards. And what is more, I know that life will not get easier as I grow older, because I already sense that there is so much to learn, so much to do. But I've found my agenda, and it is an endless list of tasks that need to be carried out on this very ordinary old homestead.

I · A REFUGE

THE OLD FARMHOUSE had been sitting empty at the end of a discontinued road for more than fifteen years. A simple hand-painted sign was nailed to the front corner, informing anyone who ventured down the road that the house was for sale. All the hunters in the area must have known about the homestead, since the land supported a healthy population of deer, rabbits, raccoons, porcupines, birds, and foxes. All the teenagers must have known about it as well, since these dirt back roads are their favorite haunts for parking, congregating, and drinking beer on warm summer nights.

The farmhouse is about a quarter of a mile in from Bonney Road, which is itself a secondary road or a back way connecting the villages of Buckfield and Sumner, Maine. I never would have known about this place if it hadn't been for my mother. She has always been a back-road explorer. She loves to head off into the woods to see what homesteads or relics of homesteads are there to be discovered. That is exactly how she found what was to become our farm in the summer of 1965. She called me in Boston, where I was living at the time, to tell me that she had found a pretty little farm for sale not far from the village where I spent my summers as a child. My mother had discovered many pieces of property for sale during her rural excursions, but this particular place she described as having a special quality. She was absolutely right.

The farmhouse was a modest yet beautifully proportioned Cape in the Greek revival style. Research into the town records showed that it had been built in 1837. Whoever repaired it last chose to paint the clapboards red on the sides of the building and white on the front and back, with white for all the trim and green for the shutters. When you approached the farmhouse, you drove along a slightly winding, narrow dirt road that faded slowly into an unused driveway. The road was so little traveled that it had a center strip of well-established weeds and grasses, and all that remained of the driveway to the barn were two courses of gravel across the lawn. Five large sugar maples, each well over a hundred years old, surrounded the farmhouse. Their enormous spreading branches made the empty house feel quite protected.

I loved the place at first sight. The farmhouse, with its forty acres (more or less), was on the market for $5000. In the mid-sixties there was still very little interest in old farmhouses in inland rural Maine. Real-estate values began to change a few years later in this part of the state, but in 1965 the prices were still low and the mortgage rate was only seven and one-half percent. It seemed very affordable, even to someone like myself who had been out of college for only three years.

Although I was born and raised in a small Maine town, I left the state in the late 1950s, never expecting to return for more than visits or vacations. After I had graduated from college, I had traveled around the United States, lived for a while in France, and returned to settle in Boston. I was just starting to make a career in the field of publishing. So when I bought the farm, I really expected to use it only as a retreat — as a place to get away from the city occasionally. It was a whimsical purchase.

Mark and I met two years later. Up until the time we were married, we made only a few trips to the country, since we were rather casually interested in the land. It was my parents who used the farm, far more often than we did. They had several small vegetable gardens here, to which we paid little attention. If we spent weekends in Maine during the summer, we usually brought along friends from Boston. When we visited during the winter months, we snowshoed in for a day or two, built fires in a couple of woodstoves, and then packed up and returned to Boston, where our lives and ambitions seemed firmly rooted.

It is so very difficult now to imagine that I was once unattached to this place. But in fact we got acquainted rather slowly. The bonds that I now have with this place have formed gradually and sometimes imperceptibly over the past twenty years. Part of that emotional journey would undoubtedly have taken place anywhere as I matured from my late twenties into my forties, but the particular choices I've made and the sensibilities I've developed have been uniquely informed by my involvement with the farm and the land and community around it.

The land that borders our property on the north and west is owned by Ruth and Linwood Bonney. Linwood's great-great-grandfather, Isaac Bonney, was one of the original settlers in the town of Sumner. During the second half of the eighteenth century, the Commonwealth of Massachusetts land office, in an effort to promote settlements in its northern territories, promised to give one hundred acres free to anyone who would clear sixteen acres in four years. This promise continued until 1784, and under it the first settlers came to this town.

During the first few years, this community was called Butterfield, after Samuel Butterfield of Dunstable, Massachusetts, one of the earliest land petitioners. Its present name, Sumner, came from Increase Sumner, who was governor of Massachusetts in

1798, when the town was incorporated. Sumner's records show that its earliest immigrants were all from Plymouth County in the Old Colony of Massachusetts. Credited as "true founders of this town" are families named Barret, Bisbee, Bonney, Bosworth, Briggs, Buck, Crockett, Cumings, Ford, Heald, Keene, Oldham, Parlin, Robinson, Stetson, Sturtevant, and Tucker. Nearly all of these names are still evident in the registry of families in Sumner and the surrounding communities.

In the centennial history of the town of Sumner, written in 1898, the earliest inhabitants are remembered in the following way:

> These early settlers of our town came of the hardy Puritan Stock which has made the name of New England famous throughout the world. A variety of circumstances tended to cultivate in them habits of thought and self restraint. Social equality and individual freedom prevailed everywhere among them; they had imbibed strong religious principals [sic] in their old Massachusetts homes, they possessed a sturdy independence, owning and tilling their own farms, and they were servants to no man. . . . The sterile soil became productive under their sagacious culture, and the barren rock, astonished, found itself covered with luxuriant and unaccustomed verdure.

The evidence of this "sagacious culture" has disappeared from most of the communities now. In our section of Maine, with few exceptions, the land has been left untilled, sold to nonfarmers, or subdivided and developed. Our neighbors, the Bonneys, now vacation on their land, coming for only a few weeks each summer. They stay in the log cabins at the end of our road, which were built in 1947, after a fire destroyed the original homestead.

Linwood and Ruth are retired schoolteachers. Linwood is in his eighties, and he is one of the most gifted oral historians I have ever met. His affection for the land and for its history is great. Were it not for his stories, it would be hard for us to imagine the vitality of Sumner's past.

According to Linwood, our farm was settled in 1837 by a family named Ellis. The building and property were sold several times; they were owned for the longest period by a family named Turner and then, before we came, by a family named Trask. The place is referred to interchangeably as the old Turner farm and the old Trask farm. The architecture of the farmhouse reflects a popular design of the time, in which the main living quarters were connected with the ells, sheds, and barns so the owners could stay under cover during the long, cold winter months, when they still had to attend to animals in the barns and haul in wood stored in the sheds. You have to live in Maine for only one snowy winter to appreciate the intelligence behind rambling New England farmhouses.

Judging by the state of the homestead when we bought it, the Trasks must have made their income only partially from the land. Apparently there were a number of children in the family, but none was interested in farming the land or in keeping the homestead. Over the years, the outbuildings were allowed to collapse, since the costs of upkeep and taxes were too high for buildings that were not needed in active agriculture. When Mr. Trask died and Mrs. Trask moved into the village of Buckfield, the house was closed up for a number of years and opened only for summer visits and occasional weekend outings. By the time we bought the farmhouse, unfortunately, only the main house and one ell remained in decent structural shape. We had to tear down the sheds and bulldoze the skeletal remains of the barns.

This was the property's history for long enough to allow alders, scrub pine, and some birch to get a good hold on the cleared land. When we arrived, there were a few visible remnants of a two-acre field and the barest hint of another eight-acre pasture.

Our forty-acre parcel is a rather hilly piece, the eastern part of which climbs steadily from an elevation of 500 feet at the house to a peak of 750 feet. Depending on the date of the topographic map that you consult, this elevation is referred to as Hedgehog Hill or Mount Oxford. All of the older neighbors use the first name. Once again, we have the Bonneys to thank for making

Hedgehog Hill available to us as it existed years ago. They gave us copies of a number of old photographs taken between 1914 and 1918. In one the viewer comes face to face with Alice Turner, standing in snowshoes atop a ten-foot pile of snow on the south lawn of the farmhouse. She stands strikingly straight and is tall and thin. I wonder if she was as stern as she appears in that picture. In another you can see Guy Turner, more weathered and plumper than his wife, collecting mail from a mailbox that is nailed to a good-sized maple tree on the front lawn. The maple was cut down long before we came, and someone planted a simple garden around its decaying stump.

In another series of photographs, taken on top of Hedgehog Hill, we encounter Linwood as a young boy, wearing handmade wooden skis, the kind that are shaped out of straight pieces of hardwood and then steamed into shape. Mark and I found a child's pair in our attic, a pair that someone abandoned before they finished steaming and curving the front tips. The photos of Linwood are dated 1914, and at that time one could stand on top of our little mountain and look in all directions down over cleared fields, sectioned off by rows of granite walls and wooded lanes. All the land was tilled, and even its steepest slopes were used for pasture.

At one time our farm hired as many as eight men to work all summer, planting, hoeing, and harvesting acres of green beans and sweet corn. Vegetables, fruits, berries, and dairy products were produced on all the neighboring farms and delivered daily to be processed or sold fresh. In Sumner there was a railroad station, part of the Portland and Oxford Central Line, from which fresh produce could be sent daily to Portland or Boston. Certain products were processed in the village in a large canning factory. There were gristmills, lumbermills, coopers, blacksmiths, and various small manufactures, often of wood products.

Linwood tells a fascinating story about the rounds that were made regularly by the community drover. This man would travel from farmhouse to farmhouse on a regular basis to buy and transport farm animals into the village, to be shipped to market. Apparently when the telephone first came into the neighborhood, around the turn of the century, the drover's arrival would always be preceded by a call from a neighbor, telling you to gather in your dogs lest they frighten the arriving herd. The call also gave you warning to prepare your animals for sale. There would then be a flurry of activity and excitement, especially among the children, who would start watching for the oncoming parade of cows, horses, sheep, goats, or whatever assortment of beasts were being brought to market.

When Linwood was born, Sumner had a population of more than a thousand people, compared with the 607 residents today. In 1900 there were nine schools, five churches with active parishes, and two grange halls, serving the eastern and western neighborhoods. The main business of the inhabitants was agriculture, including forestry, and the community was sustained by all the business and support services that contribute to agricultural activity. In the center of the village were grocery and dry goods stores, which, along with the small mills and factories, served as the center of commercial and social life.

Just a couple of miles down the road from our farm, a man named Wellington Eastman lived, worked, and published a seed catalogue as well as growing a number of the choice varieties himself. In the late 1800s, Eastman also published a sixteen-page monthly magazine called *Garden Notes*, which was available for fifty cents a year. Letters of praise came from customers not only in Maine but from as far away as Michigan and Pennsylvania.

This community portrait is in marked contrast to the Sumner that we began to visit in the 1960s. One of the oldest general stores went out of business nine years ago, after several owners struggled with declining trade. One of the two post offices closed in 1967. Only one of the granges holds on to a few members. The old gristmill, powered by the east branch of the Nezinscot River, was razed in 1937, and on its site is a small cement-block town office. The railroad line went out of service in the early 1950s, and the track bed has become a favorite trail for snowmobilers and young people with dirt bikes.

When we first came here, Mark and I occasionally hiked down over the back hill of our property, which descends steeply to the track bed and on to the river that serves as one boundary of our land. We found some decaying piles of railroad ties, and when we were lucky, we would uncover some large, rusty spikes that had been used to hold the tracks to the ties (I've kept a few spikes as paperweights and mementos). We also explored the remains of a plant that once produced bottles of spring water from Hedgehog Hill.

In listening to Linwood's stories and in reading through the collection of scrapbooks that belong to the Sumner Historical Society, I try to re-create a sense of this small town and of so many other rural New England communities. These were places that were economically self-sufficient; the families were woven together by their participation in community organizations. Children were born, grew up, and married within the area, and often stayed to continue the work of their parents.

Sumner is far from economically self-sufficient today. Its agricultural past has all but disappeared. There are few community organizations. Children often wait impatiently until they are old enough to move out of town, which they see as offering them little excitement during their teen years and no opportunity during their young working lives. It would seldom be possible for them to carry on the work of their parents, since their parents have for a long time commuted to the larger towns to find their own employment. All of the circumstances that conspired to change the agricultural nature of these villages also brought about changes in their populations. I bought a farm that was very inexpensive in the mid-sixties, but land values began to escalate as soon as the sellers found that there were lots of urban buyers out there, wanting a sane and safe refuge somewhere back in the country.

By the late sixties, more and more outsiders — which is what we will always be called — had begun to buy up old farmhouses and large parcels of land in our area. Mainers living in such small villages as Sumner and Buckfield have always held mixed feelings for outsiders. They cannot be described as hostile, nor are they exactly friendly. The kindest way of describing them would be to call them reserved. The burden of acceptance is placed on any newcomer, and out-of-towners or, worse still, out-of-staters are watched, gossiped about, judged, and even challenged for a number of years before they are welcomed into the community.

I would imagine that the integration of newcomers is made more difficult because of the insulated character of places like Sumner. This village is not really on the way from anyplace to anyplace, so it has not hosted the throngs of summer vacationers that other parts of the state have. The skiing crowds were not coming in such great numbers in the mid-sixties, and those who did come did not need to pass through our towns to get to the resorts. Thus, old farmhouses had not been redone into inns and antique barns. There were no little restaurants, and no businesses trying to capitalize on the vacationers' money.

I suppose that when we began coming more and more frequently to our rural retreat, we were seen by our neighbors as two more of those city people who had the money to buy up some of the old property. We talked faster, dressed a little differently, and showed up more and more often at the country auctions with the financial advantages that permitted us to bid up the used furniture and antiques. When we stopped in at the local grocery store and post office, we didn't linger to chat, partly because of initial shyness and lack of a common vocabulary, but partly because we were always in a hurry to get back to the farmhouse or back to the city. By the late sixties, Mark and I were meshing a pressured city schedule with a rush to get to Maine to unwind. I am certain that our urban manners were sometimes abrasive, although not intentionally so. I expected that buying goods and services could be done as quickly in Maine as my weekday transactions in Boston. It took me years to understand that when someone in rural Maine agrees to stop by when he has a chance to look at a field that needs mowing, he may mean next week or next fall. From my vantage point, I saw the local people as vague and noncommittal. From their vantage point, I must surely have seemed pushy and demanding.

As a newcomer to rural Maine, I also had a tendency to romanticize the lives I saw around me, or to oversimplify them. I was as quick to interpret simple farming methods as charming as I was slow to understand that those methods are often dictated by lack of money. As I review it now, I also feel that our ability to buy the farmhouse and land as casually as we did was a direct challenge to the families who owned the land around us. Generations of families had worked, hunted, and traveled freely over the land for nearly two hundred years. Our urban money and our more aggressive social manners gave us both an economic and a political power that was disproportionate in the area. Coastal Maine had experienced this integration of populations for a long time, since its picturesque property had been for years the summer playground of privileged urbanites. But less infiltrated sections of rural Maine were now beginning to experience these changes.

With real understanding and fondness, I now remember a couple of episodes that were meant to challenge our notion of owning the land we had purchased. The farmhouse, as I've described, is located at the end of a discontinued road, the remnants of which still meander distinctly through the woods to connect once again with Bonney Road. People from the area had played around on this road for years — hunters on foot or in their four-wheel-drive vehicles, motorcyclists and snowmobilers. A couple of years after buying the farm, we planted grass over what was part of the road immediately in front of the house. We put a log to mark the end of the road and the beginning of our new lawn, thus interrupting a well-trodden path.

Ruth Bonney visited us several times each summer while she was staying in the cabins, and on one such visit she brought along Augusta Eastman, daughter of Wellington. Augusta had recently retired as postmistress for the town of Sumner, and she lived nearby, on the Eastman homestead. The two women brought us a cake, and we were touched by the warmth of the gesture. I chose to see the gift as a sign that Ruth had decided we were all right. I also got the distinct impression that Augusta was sizing us up.

On another visit that same summer, Ruth walked up the road, stepped over our newly positioned log, and continued over the lawn to the lane back to the main road. In passing, she smiled and called out that she intended to walk that route at least once a year so that she felt it could never officially be closed to her. I will always love and respect her for choosing to instruct us so gently.

There were less gentle reminders of the feelings that we stirred by taking over the property. Several people drove their vehicles over the log and over our newly seeded lawn and virtually scoffed at us as we watched them disappear into the road through the woods. After several such encounters, we found ourselves engaged in a couple of heated confrontations that I know left small scars and bad memories. All of this now seems to have been part of an initiation, in much the way that animals sniff and display around one another when there are new individuals in a territory. Gradually, over the years, these challenges diminished and then stopped. That is not to say that we are not occasionally harassed by people who disagree with our ideas. The reasons now, however, are focused on our visibility in the community as business owners and on Mark's work as a selectman, not on our right to live here.

In the early seventies, we had lots of visitors on our land. It was not uncommon to see herds of deer in the upper fields. They came in the spring and summer to graze, and in the late summer and fall to feed on the apples that were still being produced by the abandoned orchard of standard-sized trees. Families of raccoons lived all over the property, and we would see them moving from one feeding spot to the next, an adult in the lead and a trail of babies after it. We even had a family of woodchucks, before we started farming, which played with some of our cats. We have also seen moose, bears, foxes, bobcats, grouse, and of course por-

cupines. One of the greatest pleasures in owning this piece of
land soon came from knowing that we would maintain acres of
mixed fields and woodlands, which are ideal habitats for wildlife
and birds.

For all landowners, new and old, one of the thorniest questions
rests in the decision to post the land or to leave it open to hunters.
I come from a family of talented and avid hunters. My grandparents both hunted and fished, and I remember being taken to
L. L. Bean, the Maine sporting-goods store, when my grandfather
needed to buy some new green woolen pants or a new pair of
boots. (Perhaps the memory of that very unimposing wooden
shed and my grandfather's no-nonsense New England frugality
have forever colored my current feelings for the Bean popularity.)
I also remember my parents' hunting trips to the northern part
of the state each fall, and their unsuccessful attempt to interest
me in what they called a great sport, which I felt was a real
travesty. We disagree strongly to this day, but I was so familiar
with the love of hunting that I was very aware of what posting
the land would mean to my neighbors.

When November arrived each year, I sensed a growing tension
over whether to post the land or leave the wildlife unprotected.
I have seen many new landowners move into their homesteads
and tack up KEEP OUT and NO TRESPASSING signs. These signs
have always struck me as extremely hostile and arrogant. They
disregard the history of the land's use by the community, and
they are such a visible way of imposing values by virtue of economic advantage.

After trying to sort out my conflicting feelings, I resorted to
hand-lettering signs that read NO HUNTING and nailing these to
some trees along the roadside a few days before each hunting
season. Initially the signs were stolen or destroyed. I persisted in
painting new ones, and the longer I live here, the longer the signs
are left alone. I know that I have gained some enemies, but I also
feel that I have earned some degree of ownership.

By 1971, our trips to the farm had increased so much that we were coming nearly every weekend. This was primarily because Mark began a photographic study that culminated in his first published work, *Rural Maine*, which came out from the Godine Press in 1972. It is a revealing look at our early view of the land and the people in our neighborhood.

Mark shot hundreds of rolls of film: of people, their houses, their land, their animals. Our neighborhood is in fact a constant visual mixture of old homesteads that are falling down and old homesteads that have been lovingly restored. Rural roads pass through acres of clear-cut, eroded land and then acres of carefully managed forests. Unlike coastal Maine, rural inland Maine is populated by part-time farmers, woodsmen, vacationers, and more than a handful of ex-urbanites who have pieced together some rather unorthodox careers. Whatever opportunities have lured developers into trendy Portland (and rumors promise more of the same in Lewiston and Auburn) have not yet been exploited here. As a result, the photographs in Mark's book make up a series of graphically powerful studies that look unflatteringly, but not unkindly, at faces and landscapes in an economically depressed area.

The book was well received by urban critics. It got mixed and often heated reviews from Maine people. Many Mainers had become accustomed to the countless romantic pictures of white lighthouses, calendar shots of autumn foliage and pretty white churches. One Maine magazine returned a review copy of *Rural Maine* with a letter saying that the editor and many of her colleagues felt that the book unfortunately "showed rural Maine as it really was rather than how one hoped it might be." Another letter, this one published in a local weekly, told how disgusted the reviewer felt at seeing this aspect of her community portrayed. As I look back over these photographs, and at the numerous unpublished ones in the files, I am struck by the beauty of their starkness and complexity.

Although Mark's work on his book brought us more frequently to our farm, it was not what really caught our attention while we stayed in Maine. If anything, the book and its publication, with its accompanying national reviews and gallery exhibitions, attached us more closely to our urban goals. As I look back at our first attachments to our homestead, I really remember a much more personal and seemingly insignificant activity that began in an old abandoned garden located in the furthest corner of the south lawn.

This particular corner of the land was filled with a tangle of weeds, an old forsythia bush, and many different flowering perennials and herbs. It took us several seasons even to recognize that a garden was hidden in the overgrowth. The same flowers would appear at the same time in each season, and I began to pick bouquets for the kitchen table in our apartment back in the city. I knew none of the plants by name, but from late April until late September, something or other was available from that one small area, no more than a few hundred square feet in size.

The first reference book that we bought for gardening, in an effort to help us identify some of these plants, was a simple and clearly illustrated paperback written by Mrs. William Starr Dana in 1893. She might have been writing the book while someone was puttering around in our old garden. Our edition, several times revised and illustrated, was titled *How to Know the Wild Flowers*, and it included text about and illustrations of more than a thousand flowering plants. It also included nearly every one of the plants that we had inherited in that corner.

I learned that we had blue veronica, wild columbine, tansy, achillea, wild geranium, day lilies, old-fashioned roses, physostegia, evening primrose, lily-of-the-valley, blue flag, campanula, dianthus, and fall asters. The process of identifying these plants was delightful. I began to learn how plants were classified, and a little about their historical uses, and some odd bits of information and folklore. It was a simple beginning, but one that came naturally out of our curiosity about what already existed on the property.

That first interesting information led us to notice the bushes

and flowers that were struggling to survive around the foundations of the farmhouse. On the east side of the house were lilacs,
spirea, weigelia, peonies, and hundreds of narcissus. Since little
was planted along the other sides of the building, we began to
transplant some of the bushes and perennials. As we dug and
lifted old plants out of this congestion, not only did they grow
larger and heartier, but we seemed to have released other species
from the earth. There were plants that had never before showed
themselves to us, that had apparently been lying dormant. I have
since read that many seeds can lie buried in the ground for decades and still remain viable. One example, our own evening primrose, has in fact been known to produce plants after being buried
in the soil for more than seventy years.

For several seasons we worked at reorganizing the small original garden and relocating more flowers and shrubs. In addition,
my family contributed plants from their gardens, and so did several of our neighbors, who recognized our growing interest in
plants. These contributions included violets (both purple and
white), mallow, baby's breath, aconitum, and iris. Nearly everything I've named thus far can be found around the grounds of
many old New England homesteads, a testament to their ability
to survive the climate and the uneven attention of generations
of gardeners.

Mark and I began to need more help than the Dana book could
offer, and so we started to purchase, in a really eclectic manner,
what I did not imagine would become a gardening library. At this
point in my storytelling, I am certain that veteran gardeners will
smile knowingly. But I was totally unaware of where this beginning relationship might lead me. My growing familiarity with a
place, my attachment and fondness for that place, were just starting to take hold. I didn't have the slightest inkling that this
attachment would cause me to make major changes in my life.

2 · A FIRST GARDEN

OUR TRIPS to Maine were becoming routine. Mark and I would leave Boston as soon as possible after work on Friday, trying to beat the inevitable traffic jam on Storrow Drive leading to the Mystic River Bridge. At first we returned to the city on Sunday night, but as our involvement with the farm increased, we pushed our schedule ahead to Monday morning, so that we often left Maine just before sunrise.

Those of us who make the same trips over and over develop ways of understanding and marking the distance and time of our travels. We choose signposts along the way and give these places some significance. There are places to tell you that the journey is half over. There are places that are repeatedly beautiful to come upon. There are sections of the drive that are so ugly that each time the visual assault prompts the same silent thoughts or verbalized laments. By my count, we made some 728 trips back and

forth to our farmhouse before we moved to Maine permanently.
Even now, when I drive to Boston, I remember the signposts of
our trips and inevitably repeat or reinterpret their old meanings.

In particular, I remember three landscapes, and I am certain
that these places impressed me most because they signified the
end of pieces of rural Maine. The first was a view of a very old
gambrel-roofed barn that met your eye as you rounded a curve
in the road about ten miles from our farm. As you approached
that barn, trees lined the highway on each side, so the view did
not come gradually but suddenly. When you came around the
bend in the road, that magnificent wooden building dominated
the horizon. A huge field fell steeply behind the barn, and depending on the season, you could look down at a pattern of con-
tours made by plows, harrows, or rows of fodder corn.

Now when I come around that same curve in the road, the
view is confused by a small prefabricated house that gouges a
visual hole in the foreground. The house's roof line juts up and
over the front wall and door of the barn. There are real holes in
the roof of the barn itself, and it is probably only a matter of
years before the building will begin to shift and sag on its foundations. Even though I've had many years to get used to the
new house, I am still disappointed and annoyed when I come
upon it.

There is another such view, occurring as they often do when
you come around some bend in the road. This time, the road
smoothed and straightened for a mile or so. Fields flanked both
sides, and an unusual assortment of cows were usually grazing
along the upper field, which rose slowly to another great old barn
and several other outbuildings. One corner of that field has now
been stolen for a small square house and a yard full of cars, swings,
and the paraphernalia of a young family.

The third place also includes a field and a view. In fact, the
whole area was once an enormous sixty-acre field just on the
outskirts of one of the last cities we passed through on our return
to Sumner. In the spring, there was always a vivid competition

between the grasses and the yellow dandelions. In the summer, this old pasture was a lush green, with patches of hawkweed and goldenrod. A small depression of wetland in the corner nearest the highway was filled with cattails. In the fall there were brilliant clumps of asters and Queen Anne's lace. When we were traveling that road in the winter, sometimes we would arrive in time to catch a glimpse of the sun setting over the last hill of that pasture, casting long warm shadows over the even mounds of snow.

I seldom look in that direction now, having lost interest after the bulldozers leveled the land to make way for a giant shopping mall. The stretch of highway that passes by the mall is doubly annoying, not only because it has been robbed of its view, but because it has had to accept three sets of lights to accommodate the traffic spitting in and out of the stores and other businesses that have crowded around.

Being forced to relinquish these special places no doubt increased my appreciation for all the spots that remained unchanged in a commute that Mark and I continued to make weekly for seven years. During that time, however, the most immediate and constant signpost was located only a mile away from our farm. And depending on the direction in which we were traveling, the Allen homestead was either the first or the last place we passed.

The Allens' land was settled many years before our own. The old red Cape and attached barn sit facing Bonney Road. Small plots of cleared land surround the buildings on the other three sides. The Allens were truck farmers for most of their lives, until they retired just a few years ago.

Olive Allen was a Cobb before marrying — a member of one of the original families in town. She trained to be a schoolteacher and taught in one of the old one-room schoolhouses that used to stand on the Bonney road. Her husband, Ceylon, several years her junior, was one of her pupils. After school he went away for a few years to Chicago, where he sold shoes. He returned to

Sumner and married Olive in 1941, and the couple settled on the family farm a few years later.

When we met the Allens, they were farming about three or four acres of mixed vegetables. They also had a small orchard of pear trees that produced excellent crops of Bartletts and Clapp's Favorites. In back of the barn there was a well-established bed of Latham raspberries, which were faithfully pruned of their dead canes each fall and mulched with sawdust each spring. Off and on the couple kept laying hens for their eggs, and whenever the birds stopped producing, they were used as stew meat. All of the work of the farm was done by Olive and Ceylon, with the help of Ceylon's father, Cliff, and an occasional local teenager or two who was hired on when the summer workload was at its most strenuous.

Depending on the season, the Allens tilled two or three small plots of land immediately behind their house, and they also used a couple of acres of land on the Bonney property. So we not only passed their house every day that we traveled our back road; we also saw them frequently during the farming season, when they came to their gardens on the land adjacent to ours.

If the days were very hot, or if there was a long day of picking to be done, we would hear the Allens' truck drive up our road just after sunrise. And if the air was still, as it so often is in the early morning hours, we could hear them talking and working in their garden. As time passed, we would stop by to say hello, to ask how the crops were growing, and in this way we began to get acquainted. They in turn would drop in on us, bringing some fresh vegetables or berries for us to try. The Allens never had children of their own, and early on took special interest in our comings and goings.

During the week, Olive would clip items from the local paper and save them for us. She and Ceylon began to look after our farmhouse when we were away. They came to expect a visit from us each weekend, and we from them. But even more important, Mark and I began to recognize and appreciate the seasons in terms

of the activities that went on around the Allen farmstead. As I
recall the cycle, it began in late February or March, because when
the time was right the Allens would begin to appear in their yard
after a winter of holing up indoors.

Sapping time, as any country person in New England knows,
marks the beginning of the end of winter. Whenever the days
begin to warm above the freezing mark and the nights continue
to stay cold, sap begins to flow into the branches of the sugar
maples. Ceylon would set up his barrel stove and sap pans in a
favorite spot next to the house and near the road, where he could
most conveniently haul in the wood and pails. He would have
collected small piles of slab wood for the hot fires he needed to
boil down the gallons and gallons of sap that he took from his
own trees, from the Bonney's trees, and from the great old maples
on our lawn.

During the warmth of those days, the snow would melt and
run off, forming little gullies at the edges of our road. The first
exposed ground would appear around the bases of the large lawn
maples. If the temperatures rose high enough, the sap would flow
heavily from the taps, carefully placed on the south-facing sides
of the trees. Buckets would then have to be emptied as often as
two or three times a day. Ceylon would boil down the large
amounts of sap on his outdoor stove, and as it began to thicken
into syrup, he would bring it into the farmhouse, where Olive
would finish it off in kettles on the old black Glenwood stove
in her kitchen. Then she would pack the thick amber syrup into
canning jars. The Allens kept some for their own use and sold
some, and a jar or two was usually waiting for us on our kitchen
table when we arrived Friday night.

It takes anywhere from thirty to forty gallons of sap to make
one gallon of good maple syrup. From year to year the sugar
content of the sap may change, and so a beginner is advised to
use a thermometer to be certain he has boiled his syrup to about
218 degrees before canning, or, better still, a syrup hydrometer
to make certain that the sap is reduced to the right density, so

that it will neither crystallize nor spoil after canning. The color of the sap also changes between what is called the early flows and the later ones, and although the grading of syrup for sale is based on the lightness of the color, the later collections can be just as good, albeit much darker. Ceylon and Olive always gave us jars containing the clearest amber syrup, which never misbehaved, unlike some of our own early attempts.

Just as soon as the syrup season came to a close, Olive would head out into the yard to start the outdoor spring cleaning. During the winter months the Allens piled and chopped their wood immediately in front of the porch steps. Late in March or early in April, the last of the unused wood was stored in the barn, the yard was raked, and the porch was cleared of its shovels, axes, buckets, tools, and all the rest of the winter utensils. Then Olive would start cleaning her flowerbeds, pulling away the natural mulches of leaves that had gathered and caught themselves on dried flower stalks. She had one permanent bed next to the house, and from year to year a new little bed of spring flowers would appear somewhere in the yard. On our trips every weekend we would look for the first hyacinths, tulips, or daffodils to appear in her gardens. We could judge by the Allens' flowers that our own gardens would be in bloom a week or two later, because the Allen farm is on the southern slope of Hedgehog Hill; our land flows down over the northern slope.

From the end of April on, all the outdoor activities revolved around preparing the land to be farmed again that season. The Allens never owned a tractor, so they hired Eddie Trask to come do their plowing and harrowing. Eddie had a small old Farmall cub, which he would drive up from the center of Sumner village to plow for the Allens and for the Bonneys. Linwood and Ruth opened up their log cabins each spring when Linwood felt that it was time to plant his peas. So when Eddie Trask appeared in the neighborhood, we knew the gardening season was officially under way.

The beauty of newly plowed and harrowed fields is as appealing to me now as it was in those first few years. Neatly rolled furrows of rich brown earth hold such promise. The land is always moist when it is first worked, so that the color of the soil is darkest then. Once the plowing was completed, Eddie would hook up his set of disc harrows and spend hours on each garden plot, riding up and down and across the furrows, chewing up the soil and smoothing it out in preparation for planting. The cowbirds and robins, which were also back in our area in great numbers and variety at that time of year, ran along after the tractor, picking insects and worms out of the newly worked earth.

Like most of our neighbors, and like many other truck farmers I would later come to know, the Allens grew none of their own seedlings. They always relied on a local greenhouse grower to do that for them. I always thought that that was rather strange, since Olive could grow the healthiest collection of houseplants on the tops of bureaus and on stands pushed up to every available window in her house. But I suppose that was for fun; vegetable seedlings were for money, and the Allens were not about to gamble at the outset of the season.

Sometime in the middle of May, Ceylon and Olive would pick up their greenhouse seedlings and we would see rows of old-fashioned wooden flats set along the porch railing, where the plants had been placed to harden off. The Allens judiciously prepared their plants for the transition from the protected environment in which they had been grown to the rigors of the fields. They needed the earliest crops they could manage and took every precaution, hardening off gradually and planting on overcast days to avoid setting back the plants' production. Regardless of the crop (with the one exception of peas), farmers in our area waited for Memorial Day to set out their tender seedlings. They also often waited until that time to direct-seed crops like corn, beans, and squashes.

In this part of the world, unless you own land in a cold valley or river bottom, you can count on the nights to be frost-free from the end of May to the middle of September. It turns out to be great good fortune that Mark and I happened to land on a farm on the side of a mountain. Only a mile away, and three hundred feet lower, there can be frosts in May, sometimes in June and August, and most certainly in early September, whereas it is not uncommon for us to have all of May and all of September without a frost. Anyone contemplating buying a piece of land does well to inquire about the climate of that particular area, since conditions can vary so much from one hill to the next. We have acquaintances in the nearby village who are restricted to growing only cold-weather vegetables for sale, since they can never count on a summer long enough to mature even the shortest-season tomatoes and peppers.

Tomatoes were always one of the Allens' main income vegetables. During the growing season, all of their time was occupied with planting, cultivating, harvesting, and marketing their produce. The work was done either by hand or with the help of a single workhorse. Ceylon would have a different horse from one year to the next. In the spring he bought the animal from someone who had used it to skid or haul out logs, and in the fall he sold it back to a woodsman. That way, the Allens didn't have the work or expense of stabling a horse through the winter. One year we would see a chestnut gelding out in the pasture next to the house; the following year it might be an old gray mare.

Planting with horse-drawn implements usually required two people — sometimes Ceylon and his father, but more often Ceylon and Olive. Ceylon would drive the harnessed horse, walking with reins in hand beside the animal; Olive would steer the single-row corn planter. This was a wonderfully simple old tool, with a furrow maker in the front, a hopper for carrying, releasing, and spreading granular fertilizer directly in the rows, and a smaller hopper that dropped seeds at distances determined by settings on the top of the planter. The implement also had two blades for covering the seeds and a roller for tamping everything into place.

Cultivating was also handled by the horse and two workers. Ceylon would drive the animal while Olive would try to steer, maneuvering the tines of the cultivator between the rows of young plants. Depending on the temperament of the horse, the strength of the person on the tines, and the smoothness of the ground, this work can proceed in a number of ways. One year Ceylon found himself a bargain horse that had worked in the Canadian woods, and if it understood anything at all — a point I'm not willing to testify to — it had to be directed in French. The Allens were a little short on French, and when Ceylon tried to guide the horse through two dense rows of healthy potato plants, the animal got out of control and Olive cultivated up a section of small tubers to the music of Ceylon's blaspheming. There were actually lots of variations on that scene, and I was surprised that the horse made it through the summer.

Week after week, we would watch our neighbors work and see the changes in the developing gardens as the vegetative cover thickened and deepened in color. By midsummer the produce would start to ripen: peas first, followed by beans, cukes, tomatoes, carrots, beets, corn, and then the squashes and pumpkins.

The Allens marketed most of their produce directly from the back of a 1962 baby-blue Dodge van, which Olive drove around through the residential sections of nearby communities. Often she would leave early in the morning and return in the late afternoon, having made the rounds of her customers and emptied out the contents of the truck in the process. Whatever was left over or picked between delivery days the Allens would display in peck and bushel baskets in their front yard. Passersby could stop and buy whatever was in season. In addition to selling, Olive canned hundreds of quarts of food for the upcoming winter. She made relishes, pickles, and jams and processed yellow and green beans, sweet corn, tomatoes, and peas. She also dried bean seeds in the house, behind one of the farm's woodstoves. Some of the seeds were stored for cooking, and some were kept for planting next season.

During the summer, the flowers in the front gardens would continue to change. To the perennial beds, Olive would add her favorite annuals — marigolds, petunias, and always verbena. They bloomed all summer, along with her prized gold-banded lilies, the gloriosa daisies, and the tiger lilies. By the time the rose and yellow chrysanthemums dominated the garden, I knew that summer was on the wane.

In late September, the squashes would be hauled up onto the porch to "heal"; once their outer skins had thickened and toughened, they were ready to be stored away for the winter. The pears would be picked. The horse would disappear from the pasture, and the woodpile would begin to grow on the front lawn of the farmhouse. In the fall, Olive spent quite a bit of time splitting and carrying in wood for the kitchen stove. She always said that she loved the work because it kept her in shape.

And then one weekend, inevitably, we would drive up the road to our farm, and there would be the first snow, covering the fields. Only the dried-out corn stubble and tall weeds would be visible above the white cover, and the outdoor activities of our neighbors would draw to a close for the winter.

In 1972 Mark and I planted our first vegetable garden. Since we didn't have the vaguest notion of how to go about it, we went to the Allens and asked them if they would help us out. They seemed both flattered and amused, but were quite willing to give us as much guidance as we needed.

The only thing that I could anticipate having to do was clear the land for cultivation. The most easily reclaimable field lay about seventy-five yards in front of the farmhouse, and it had grown up with alders, poplars, white pine, and a few undistinguished bushes. For several weekends we cut and hauled brush, felled a few pines, and tried to pull out roots and rocks with chains attached to the frame of our first farm truck, a rugged old green half-ton Chevrolet pickup. I had never worked this hard physically in my whole life. By the end of each workday, I ached all over. My hands developed calluses and blisters, and I had bruises over my face and forearms where branches had snapped back or slipped when I was hauling brush. Despite those complaints, though, the project was more satisfying and the rewards more immediate than anything I could imagine. We began with a rather untidy old field, and in a couple of weeks we had brushpiles ready to be burned and a small piece of land ready to be plowed.

The Allens got Eddie Trask to come with his tractor to plow for our first garden. The land was very difficult to work — it was still rough and cluttered with pieces of roots and stones — but once the tractor was able to turn over the first clean furrow, the plot began to yield. I can appreciate now the difficulty of working a tractor. It takes real skill and concentration to make certain that the tip of the plow blade catches the soil and turns it up and over. You have to watch constantly to make certain that the furrows roll over, burying the sod under fresh soil so that the vegetation will begin to decompose. Mr. Trask was very skilled on his small machine, and he managed to work up an area about an acre in size. That was the amount of space the Allens had instructed us to get ready, and we had no idea that this was perhaps more than a couple needed for a first garden.

The lightweight Farmall cub could handle the plowing, but it did not have the necessary weight to harrow the land. Its discs could not cut fresh sod, so we were advised to seek out the help of another neighbor, who owned a larger set of harrows. This time the work was done not by machine but by a pair of Belgian workhorses.

That was the first time that I saw Ellery Corson and his team at work. He used the animals in the woods during the winter months, and in the fields or in pulling contests at the fairs for the rest of the year. You have to know that Ellery stands about five-foot-six and weighs no more than 140 pounds. The horses each stood a foot taller and weighed a total of one and a half tons. Once he had his horses under harness, however, you didn't notice that the man was so much smaller than his animals, because he worked them beautifully. I can re-create clear images of him

driving the team for hours over our field. The harrows chewed
and bumped over the furrows, cutting away at the sod, the roots,
and the loose earth, and Ellery had to stop every few hundred
feet to toss rocks and debris out of his way. Such pictures of him
at work don't necessarily belong in this century. There were no
machinery sounds, only the calls of a human voice, the scraping
of the discs against the land, and the snorting of the animals.

When he finished, I remember, he half-apologized for not being
able to smooth out the soil any more. As far as we were concerned, he had prepared the land for planting well beyond the
capabilities of most machinery. Some large rocks could not be
moved without large equipment, and a number of roots would
not yield to the blades of the harrows. Even if I had then known
about the powerful tractors and tillers that can pulverize such
soil, I would never have given up the opportunity of watching
the beauty of one man with a pair of horses. It made me recall
the contract agreement that many such men had made almost
two hundred years ago — to clear sixteen acres in four years, in
exchange for settling on the land. All the big rocks sitting peace-
fully in the stone walls in rural Maine had been wrestled out of
the earth and moved on drags by teams of horses or oxen. All
these miles of stone walls are reminders of the back-breaking
labor that had originally prepared these fields for agriculture.

Once the piece of land was harrowed, Mark and I spent another
few weekends trying to remove some more pieces of roots and
stumps. We collected piles of stones and what rocks we could
carry and dumped the piles into a clearing, so that vehicles could
drive from the road into the field. According to the Allens, we
were now ready to begin planting, but when I looked over that
rough rectangle of brown earth, I felt fairly skeptical. I asked Cliff
over and over whether he really thought anything would grow
in that soil. He kept reassuring me that we would have a good
garden, and not to worry.

Ceylon brought us his workhorse, and we used the planter to
mark out the rows and spread granular fertilizer. The first things

that we planted were hills of squash and cucumbers. Our neighbors filled their hands with seeds and showed us how to drop three or four of them in each hill, cover them over, and tamp down the earth with a hoe. We followed along after them, and part way down each row they passed us the seeds and hoes and talked us through the remainder of the planting.

Then we hitched the horse to the planter and seeded five rows each of beans and corn. Every few feet the planter bumped into rocks and roots, so we had to stop, clear the space, pile the debris at one side of the garden, and then start the horse again. It took us the rest of the weekend to finish the seeding.

The next weekend we set out some of the small seedlings that our neighbors had chosen for us. There were tomatoes, cabbage, and broccoli. Last, we were instructed how to cut up potatoes, leaving at least two eyes in each piece, and how to drop the pieces into trenched rows, leaving about a foot between each piece. Once this planting was done, we stared out over an acre of bare dirt with a few rows of small, rather helpless-looking seedlings that took their first beating from some hot sun, winds, and a few flea beetles. I was really doubtful that anything would come of all the work, and left for the city that Sunday evening with few expectations.

During that week in Boston, I told some friends about the project, but then I got absorbed in the business of designing a magazine and didn't give the garden much thought until Friday. Mark and I left the city in time to reach Maine before dark. Before carrying anything into the house, we headed over to the field. It was all there. The seedlings had survived and actually put on a little size. Even more thrilling, there were rows of little green leaves nearly everywhere we had planted, with the exception of the potatoes; they took another week or so to show their first growth above ground.

We examined the small plants. The leaves were different in each row, but we couldn't identify a thing. We called the Allens, and they came up first thing Saturday morning to tell us what

was germinating. Our rural education was beginning. We were
starting to identify patterns of plants in their early growth, and
our teachers were amused but reassuring.

The thrill of watching a newly seeded row push up through
the soil never diminishes. In fact, the thrill probably increases
over the years, as the farmer becomes able to anticipate and
appreciate the stages of growth and production. Now I can look
over new growth and watch as the first cotyledons develop true
leaves. I can distinguish the endless variations of green, yellow-
green, blue-green that are keys to identifying the plants. I can
gaze across a garden and gauge the time of year by the relationship
of green space to brown space, as the earth is constantly being
covered by developing plants.

But in that first season, all that was unimaginable. The summer continued with a step-by-step explanation of the stages of
seeding, planting, cultivating, hoeing, hilling, thinning, staking,
and harvesting. All of these terms had very little meaning to me
in the beginning; the complex interrelationship of one task and
the next took seasons to understand and apply. So Mark and I
quite simply relied on our teachers to tell us what to do next.
We were very fortunate to have the Allens — they were generous
and enthusiastic, and I suppose it really was a pleasure for them
to have two young people so interested in their lifetime skills.
Over the years, our attitudes about soils, fertilizers, pesticides,
varieties of plants, and farming methods changed, causing us to
have very different opinions from theirs. But that didn't matter
in that first season.

We shared the workhorse with the Allens for that summer and
the next. Often I would get up very early on Saturday morning,
dress, eat, and then walk down through the woods road that
connected our property with theirs. We would harness the horse,
and I would climb on its back and ride it through the woods to
our field. Then Mark and I would cultivate the rows for hoeing,
or use discs to hill up the rows of beans, corn, and potatoes.

When it came to weeding and hoeing, the elder Mr. Allen was

our principal teacher. Cliff was masterful with a hoe, a skill I had never even valued until I tried to make the hoe work the way he did. At eighty, he could still maneuver the tool around for hours, picking off weeds, thinning out a hill of squash, or hilling up a row of young potatoes. He knew how to take advantage of the loose soil to smother weeds and support the stems of desirable plants. I've watched him work an entire row without bending down to do any of the operations with his hands. To this day, when we hire new people to work in the fields, I watch them underestimate the skill one needs to hoe a piece of land for hours on end. The abilities to use tools efficiently, to work for hours and conserve energy, and to pace oneself accurately are all essential skills that take years to develop.

Our first garden grew wonderfully well. There were not many weeds in the newly turned piece, and even fewer insects. Fortunately for us, the Allens were rather conservative in their use of chemical sprays, so we didn't get much instruction that we would later have to rethink or abandon. They did teach us to use granular fertilizer, and that was how we fed our plants for a couple of years. But the most significant thing about that first garden was its size, and ultimately its yield.

We were swamped with vegetables. We ate what we could and gave food away to our families, friends, and neighbors — at least to those few who did not have their own gardens. In the end we searched around for anyone, friend or stranger, who could use the food. We hauled bushels of produce back to Boston to give away. We also began to learn how to put food by.

My parents were amused when we began to can our vegetables, and reminded me that we had always had a pantry full of canned vegetables, pickles, and jams when I was growing up. My childhood was spent in a house built by my great-grandfather. When I was a child there, my parents and my grandparents were living together. My grandmother canned food and taught my mother how to do the same. Now it was my mother's turn to teach me. When I asked her for help in processing food at the farm, not only did she have old family recipes, she still had boxes of the family's old blue-tinted canning jars. Some had rubber ring tops, and a few had the old enamel and tin covers stamped with names such as Lightning, Atlas, Clark's Peerless, Ball, and Mason. (All our Kerr jars with their screwtop metal covers I have since purchased at the farmers' union.)

Mark was reminded by his family that in Russia, where they lived until the late 1950s, they had stored vegetables in deep pits for the winter. They had salted and pickled cabbages with apples and carrots and kept them in wooden barrels. So with recipes and advice from our families and some contributions from our neighbors, we began to experiment with ways of storing our garden produce. The first results were extremely uneven, but there were enough successes to keep our enthusiasm going.

We began by making all kinds of pickles, jams, and jellies, green tomato mincemeat, and sauerkraut. The last two items were very good, and that fall and winter we gave away gifts from our own pantry. Because some of our attempts failed, we searched for good books and pamphlets that would help us avoid problems, primarily with food spoilage. The Department of Agriculture (USDA) produces a number of good and inexpensive publications that are frequently updated, and the state university extension services are also a useful source of information. I still scan the latest bulletins from the extension service, because canning techniques have to be constantly reviewed as the chemical makeup of vegetables changes with repeated hybridization.

Over the past fifteen years, our canning, freezing, storing, and drying of food has continued to go through revision and refinement. We are always weeding out the good recipes from the disappointing ones. We are also better able to gauge how much and what kinds of food we will need for a season. For years we ended up with dozens of jars of one kind of relish and twice as many freezer bags of one vegetable as we could use. By the end of any season now, between our own efforts and those of my parents, we have a pantry filled with an array of beautifully colored and labeled jars. The freezer comes close to being emptied just as it's time to put in the new crops of peas and the chopped rhubarb for next winter's pies. In a carefully planned season, the potatoes in the root cellar supply us for most of the winter, and a few tubers which we will use to plant another crop are left over. (I think that it might not have taken us so long to plan our food needs if we had kept some notes on the quantities and kinds of things we stored.)

As that first summer of gardening drew to an end, we were more than delighted with the results, both in food and in experience. We harvested the last of our crops and had the acre plowed in the fall. We hoped that the winter and spring would hasten the rotting of the roots and stumps that had plagued us during that first season. We didn't know that each spring would bring to the surface a new crop of rocks, constantly pushed up by the heaving frosts.

The snows came and covered the field, and we moved back inside the farmhouse for the weekends. With one year of gardening to our credit, we set plans in motion for the next season. I borrowed a copy of *Horticulture* magazine from the Buckfield library, and sat down with it and a stack of postcards. I scanned each page of that winter issue and systematically wrote away for every seed and garden catalogue that the issue mentioned. In a matter of a few weeks, we arrived at the farm on Friday nights to find our mailbox stuffed with pamphlets, booklets, brochures, and direct-mail offers.

I can think of nothing that is more helpful to the beginning gardener than to read through all the gardening catalogues that are produced. Back in the early seventies, most of these publications were free, but even today, when many companies ask for only a dollar or two, the information they offer makes the price well worth it. A good stack of gardening catalogues can provide you with reading matter for many a winter evening. Good catalogues offer common and botanical names of plants, photographs and/or illustrations in black and white or color, and cultural information. A few offer historical information and assistance in planning garden layouts and space. After only a few seasons, it is easy for the user to discriminate between those catalogues that are trying to sell with accurate information and those that probably overstate the capabilities of their seeds, plants, or tools. I have kept a library of many of our original mailings, which I still use for reference.

Our first vegetable garden had been very basic, and was based on the plans of truck farmers who grew those crops that were the most dependable and marketable. It was an excellent beginning and a good point of departure. But now I wanted to choose our own seeds and to expand the variety of food we grew. There is nothing that can assist your imagination so well as piles of seed catalogues in February. I don't need to explain this to seasoned gardeners. And there is no point in warning new gardeners to be realistic and selective in ordering seeds and plants for the upcoming season. From that first year on, there has never been any doubt in my mind that next year's garden will be more ambitious.

3 · APPRENTICESHIP

WE TACKLED our second vegetable garden with the confidence of true sophomores. Preparing the land was considerably easier because most of the small brush and roots had rotted beneath the winter snow, and the previous summer of cultivation meant that there was little remaining sod. Once again we hired other farmers to do the plowing and harrowing. We now had at least some idea of the order in which work was done. As with any new undertaking, one of the first hurdles to overcome was the acquisition of a working vocabulary. The previous season had provided us with names of tasks, tools, machinery, and plant varieties, and with ways of talking about the weather that are peculiar only to farmers.

If memory serves me well, the Allens had a chestnut gelding that year. They expected us to borrow their horse again, and they were prepared to advise us through another season. They ordered extra flats of tomato, pepper, cabbage, and broccoli plants for us, but we chose our own seeds from a variety of companies that we had become acquainted with over the winter. We added a number of vegetables to our garden, including melons, onions, cauliflowers, summer squashes, radishes, and beans for drying. We did not, however, cut down very much on the amounts of our first-year plantings, so by July we began harvesting prodigious amounts of vegetables. We bought a freezer and began to freeze and can even more of our crops than we had the year before. There was still a surplus of food.

One weekend late in June, a neighbor called to tell us that she heard on the radio about a farmers' market that was being organized in Lewiston, only twenty miles from our farm. She thought we might be interested. Quite on impulse, I called the Cooperative Extension Service that was heading up the effort, and I was told that the first market was open to anyone who had his or her own produce to sell. The markets would begin in two weeks, on Saturday mornings at seven-thirty, in a parking lot donated by one of Lewiston's Franco-American snowshoe clubs. Mark and I decided to go.

About eight vehicles showed up for that first market. We were quite a collection. In addition to Mark and me, there were full-time truck farmers, retired mill workers who were farming part-time, weekend gardeners, and a couple of craftspeople, since the first market was billed as a combination farmers' and crafters' market. The vehicles were as varied as the sellers, ranging from station wagons carrying a few baskets of vegetables to three-quarter-ton pickups with hundreds of pounds of produce. Since there was no prearranged market plan, we stationed our vehicles on a first-come, first-serve basis. After everyone had arrived, we were randomly positioned in a gravel parking lot, fenced in by a tall chain-link fence and overshadowed by a huge billboard. The early morning sun cast some thankful relief on that rather dingy spot.

Mark and I were two of the first to arrive, because we had so little to sell that it had taken us no time to prepare our truck. We had picked most of the vegetables the evening before and outfitted our truck with an assortment of wooden apple crates and pieces of plywood, from which we made a display table. We arranged our goods on the table and marked each item with a quickly lettered price card. You could sense a certain amount of tension on that first market day: each farmer was eyeing the others, wondering what the others had brought, what they would charge, and if there would be enough customers to make the trip worthwhile. Most of the other sellers had a history of selling from their trucks, much as Olive had done. Some had sold produce to local supermarkets and restaurants when they could. This was the first attempt in our area to bring farmers together to cooperate while they were simultaneously competing against one another.

Customers began arriving even before we were able to finish setting up. In a matter of one and a half hours, Mark and I had sold all of our extra garden produce for $18.75. We were absolutely delighted. The relationship of the money to the effort it had taken to acquire it had no influence on our reactions; the pleasure came entirely from the experience of producing something tangible and then selling it directly to the consumer. Other farmers also sold all of their produce, and there was an air of excitement and optimism that seemed to be shared by sellers and buyers alike. After packing our truck with empty baskets, boxes, and boards, we headed back to the farm, making plans for the next Saturday market.

That same afternoon Mark and I walked up and down the rows of our garden, trying to evaluate the plantings so that we could see what might be ready for harvest by the end of the week, for the second market. And so it went for the next seven weeks. Our weekly sales grew from $18.75 to an all-time high of $61.34 during the middle of August, when all the crops were producing heavily. At the final day of the market in September, we took in $49.38.

During the heaviest production in August, we had more cucumbers, summer squashes, and cabbage than we could sell at the farmers' market, so we brought our produce to a small grocery store where we often bought supplies. The buyer agreed to take our vegetables. Then, at the end of the season, we exchanged twelve bushels of potatoes for sixty dollars' worth of milk from a neighbor's dairy. According to my records, our last sale was made on November 1, when we earned $11.31 for some parsnips and turnips. When we added everything together, we discovered that we had taken in $498.43 from our second garden.

Our entry into the vegetable-selling business was just this casual and simple. Moreover, we counted every penny of income as real profit, and in the most naive sense, I suppose, it was. Those vegetables would have been given away or discarded if we had not sold them. The naive belief that anything that can be sold is profit would continue to play an ever-increasing role in our notions about farming for a living. But since we were not forced to look at the expenses of farming, in that summer of 1973, we never complicated the questions of pricing, profits, and losses. We were not at that time a family that needed to sustain itself on an agricultural income.

I am able to report our first sales figures to the exact penny because I began taking notes on our selling activities at the outset. I go back now to the first set of records we ever had, notes gathered in an old spiral-bound college notebook left over from one class or another. I continued to use the same notebook for the next four years, until all of its pages were filled, some with statistical data and others with random narrative information. This record keeping, started out of mild curiosity, has been the underpinning of all the business growth and whatever successes we have had. As the years progressed, the notes became more deliberate and more detailed. The weeks of selling were numbered, the crop prices were included, and the field space devoted to crops was noted. I began to include information on the weather, the harvest dates for the crops, the peak seasons for production and sales. I included a sentence or two about how the weather or holidays affected the crowds at the markets. I gathered some of the information just for its sentimental value, and it has been enjoyable and amusing to reread dates for and comments on setting out the grape arbor, trenching and planting one hundred asparagus roots, and transplanting two young maples to the newly planted lawn on the west side of the farmhouse.

After only a couple of years of keeping a journal, I could begin to see some progress in the sales of our crops, and I realized that data collection was becoming increasingly important. But our rather compulsive record keeping was often the subject of ridicule and criticism at the farmers' market. Other sellers seemed overly aware of our note taking, and we were asked by many members why we bothered to record each and every sale. We were told that it was ridiculous to try to write down information when the crowds were heavy and we were trying to wait on people. Numerous older farmers at the markets said that they knew how much they planted and approximately how much they made. The challenge for them lay principally in having the earliest crops of the favorite fruits and vegetables — they were competing to have the first corn, tomatoes, cucumbers, beans, and apples. Beyond that, there was very little sophistication in the marketing strategies of most of our peers in those early days.

Despite the criticism we received, I knew instinctively that we needed real information to remind us of our summer's activities, information that we could interpret in planning for the years ahead. There was an additional reason for my tenacity in record keeping. Mark and I were new and part-time growers, with no plans to give up our city lives. Our farming was limited to weekends and summer vacations, and even at the outset, I was interested in seeing how a finite amount of time and space given to gardening could be managed to yield the best produce and income. Each year, during the winter months — time we now refer to as farming on the kitchen table — Mark and I would study our notes, evaluate the same one-acre plot of cultivated land, count out its rows, estimate the hours of time we would have to work the land, and try to come up with a plan that would give us the greatest returns. We were asking not only for more income but for the opportunity to learn about new vegetable varieties. It became important to be able to compare the relationship of space, costs, and time, because we were having to mete out our energies carefully, divided as we were between urban and rural activities.

Although most of the other sellers at the market may not have shared our belief in record keeping, there were a few who recognized the sincerity of our interest in market gardening. As it turned out, they were the most successful growers among the membership, and they became our teachers, along with the Allens.

As the market grew in membership and popularity, each of us adopted a permanent location, and so Clarence Bradbury became our constant Saturday neighbor. Clarence, who had retired to Maine from Connecticut, where he had operated a junkyard, was one of the first members of the Lewiston farmers' market. He farmed about twenty acres of land and specialized in growing tomatoes. Regardless of the season, he always had the first ripe fruit for sale, and over the years many of us tried to challenge his lead. None of us ever succeeded.

Raising early tomatoes was only one of Clarence's skills, however. He paid a great deal of attention to marketing. Regardless of the weather or the time of year, Clarence was the first seller to arrive at the market, so that he would have plenty of time to arrange his produce in an attractive display before the early morning shoppers came. Some of the other producers (almost always the less successful ones) would drive their trucks into place once the market was under way, and they never got properly set up for the day. Some members would fail to show up on a stormy Saturday, or they would not bother to come for the earliest and latest marketing dates, when their gardens were not producing heavily. But Clarence always came, and always arrived first.

Not only was the Bradbury display the most attractive; the Bradbury display had the best salesman. Clarence loved to sell, or so it appeared. He worked very hard with each potential customer. If he could catch the attention of a passerby, he would engage him or her in conversation about the weather, the quality of his food, his farm, why he chose to raise the particular varieties that he did. He would give customers information about using the food. Inevitably, during the conversation he would bag up a pound of this or that. He never sat on the tailgate of his truck waiting for someone to ask him a question. His manner was friendly and persuasive. Even when he didn't have a customer in front of his stand, he kept busy arranging and adjusting his display. He is one of the few farmers I have known who put as much effort into selling his wares as into growing them.

Fortunately, Clarence took it upon himself to instruct Mark and me. Frequently he would walk over to our truck and ask us how we were doing. He showed us how to keep a product selling by constantly moving it into smaller and smaller boxes, so that the last of the food still looked plentiful as it mounded up over the top of its container. "You can never sell the last of anything if it is sitting in the bottom of a big box," he warned us repeatedly. He gave us advice on vegetable varieties, pointing out that some were more reliable than others in our climate. He suggested some varieties that had more eye appeal than others. He critiqued our display, reminding us to set up alternating colors and shapes of produce — a criticism that embarrassed me, a designer from Boston, working on a national magazine: I had forgotten to apply some basic design principles to my own wares.

Bud Wallace also attracted a substantial following at the earliest farmers' markets. He was the first member of the group to advertise that he farmed organically. He was, in fact, one of the earliest members of the organic farmers' movement in Maine. Lest you picture him as a hirsute, barefooted young back-to-the-lander, let me inform you that Bud was a chain-smoking, clean-shaven, baseball-cap-wearing fifty-year-old who, like Clarence, retired to Maine from Connecticut. He was also an informed horticulturalist and, like Clarence, generous with advice for newcomers.

Bud was perhaps the most intellectually curious farmer in the group, a man who was constantly trying and evaluating new varieties and new planting methods. He was aggressively interested in improved farming techniques, and welcomed both academic and field information that would support the growth of his farm. He was one of the few farmers we had met at that point who was always reading reports from the agricultural experimental stations, attending meetings and seminars. He also gave lectures to groups of farmers and home gardeners, and has since gone on to teach courses for the state university.

We often consulted Bud when we ran into problems, but there was one time in particular when we called the Wallace farm in a state of panic. Mark and I had been lured by one or another of the gardening magazines that promised unheard-of profits, and we decided to raise a partial acre of onions from sets. We ordered four bushels, or one hundred and twenty pounds of sets, which translates into thousands and thousands of tiny onion bulbs, each the size of a dime. The sets arrived by truck, and we waited for the first suitable gray, cool, misty day to start our planting. We headed out into the field with the four bushels, thinking that we could plant everything in part of one day. Working on our knees, we inched our way down the rows, painstakingly pushing each bulb into the soil, being careful to space them evenly and to point them right side up.

Some eight hours and three aching backs later (we had help that time), we had managed to plant only one of the bushels of bulbs. We were so frustrated that we figured there must be some secret to this whole process that we didn't understand, so that evening I called Bud. No, Bud didn't know of any other way to do it. So the next day we carried out only one bushel to plant.

After four days of planting on our hands and knees, the entire undertaking went from bad to worse. The weeds grew faster than we could control them with mechanical and hand cultivation, and by the end of the season we had five-foot-tall pigweed, knots of witchgrass, and onions not much larger than the bulbs we had originally put in. Years later, Bud remembered our call for help and revised his response, having learned himself that it is possible to drop sets quickly into shallow furrows, cover them, and tamp them down mechanically. The little bulbs will quite nicely sprout upwards to produce onions. As for the weed problems, Bud could write volumes.

Just recently I learned that the Wallace farm will be conducting some experiments on the allelopathic properties of plants that could work as natural herbicides. The notion is that some crops inhibit the growth of other plants. If they were planted in some specific succession, then the soil would contain natural ingredients that keep certain weeds from growing. We look forward to the results of Bud's work over the next few years. I also hope that there will be continuing pressure to support research for problems that plague organic gardeners.

Many of the farmers we became acquainted with at the market had rather sizable amounts of acreage under cultivation. They were farming seven days a week on homesteads that had lots of cleared fields. In our case, the limits on our time to garden and the small space that we had for growing pressed us into thinking about farming in a particular way. Our acreage was very hilly, and most of the land, even if it was cleared, would not be suitable for row cropping. At most we could claim about ten acres for tillage. We had begun gardening by clearing the easiest old field, and that effort had proved to us that clearing land was not only difficult but costly. But even if we had had acres of flat fields, I am not certain that we would simply have continued to plow up more and more land each season.

The challenge to us, as we saw it, was to coax small spaces into great productivity. That goal, defined early, has continued with us until this day. It has undergone scrutiny at the same time as we have looked at issues of economy and the aesthetic development of our farm. Each person who chooses to raise crops ultimately has to find a scale for the operation that matches a whole range of expectations.

Fortunately, both Mark and I have always been hungry for new information, and we began augmenting our field experience with as much reading about matters horticultural as we could afford. We began to collect books, reprints, brochures, textbooks, and catalogues. We went to libraries and bookstores, and wrote away to companies and manufacturers on subjects ranging from vegetable gardening to beekeeping. At any given time, the reading material stacked up on my bedstand includes novels, newspapers, magazines, and scores of gardening manuals.

As it turned out, some of the most useful information for our particular purposes came from horticultural books produced during the latter half of the nineteenth century and the early part of the twentieth. In those days, farms were diverse operations, and the work was performed primarily by family members or a few hired hands. Land was maintained by careful cultivation and with animal fertilizers available from the farms themselves, and the plots were usually small and planted in rotation. Large-scale monoculture and chemical farming were not yet the predominant methods. Many of the leading positions of organic farming groups today are articulated soundly in the farming manuals of previous generations.

One of my favorite old textbooks, titled *Farm Management*, by G. F. Warren, opens with a preface that reads:

> Long ages of experience and a generation of scientific research have resulted in a fund of popular knowledge on how to raise crops and animals. But there is less background of tradition concerning business methods on the farm, and colleges have given little attention to this kind of problem. The success of the individual farmer is as much dependent on the application of business principles as it is on crop yields and production of animals.

An interesting excerpt, given the fact that it was written in 1913. Oddly enough, for the past two years the Maine Department of

Agriculture has begun to focus on the need to educate the state's agricultural producers to become more astute businesspeople and marketers. Special funds have been allocated for seminars in using computers on the farm, assessing marketing opportunities, and looking at farm crops for their value-added potential.

Despite the proliferation of gardening books with handsome covers and full-color illustrations, I would be loath to part with a very utilitarian-looking text produced in 1912 by Ralph L. Watts, dean and director of the School of Agriculture and Experimental Station of the Pennsylvania State College. There are chapters on soils, animal manures, green manures and cover crops, the construction of hot beds, cold frames, and greenhouses. I mention only a few, because I am struck by his attitude in the chapter on insect enemies and diseases, which reads:

> Spraying is often necessary, but it is expensive and should not be employed ordinarily until all other practical means of prevention have failed. Single cropping or the want of proper rotation frequently causes trouble. When a crop pays unusually well, the temptation is to continue its cultivation upon the same ground for years — a practice which harbors insects and diseases. . . .
>
> When plants are kept in a thrifty condition there is reduced danger of serious loss from both insects and diseases. Judicious fertilizing, cultivating and watering may be worth far more in warding off attacks than any amount of spraying.

These two reference works — Warren's and Watts's books — offer over one thousand pages of information and advice, well indexed and in most cases as current as I want. I found each of these for under a dollar at a used-book sale. Admittedly, people have different motives for buying books, and even when we are marshaling our funds very carefully, we almost never feel that we cannot afford a book on gardening that offers some new bit of information or an opinion that will be helpful. And since I have become so indiscriminate a collector, I can offer only a somewhat eclectic list of suggested reading in the bibliography at the end of this book. Still, the list might be of some help, if not in its specific titles, then by its suggestion that there are a number of ways in which to be interested in gardening.

Our enthusiasm for literature on farming was not always shared by our neighbors or by members of the farmers' market. When we referred in conversation to something we had learned by reading, we were often chided for our basic belief in "book learning," as it was called. There were repeated variations on the opinion that farmers do not write books; it is just those professors at the agricultural schools who write, but they don't actually run farms. This strong prejudice made us cautiously edit our conversations with many of our rural peers. We were also criticized for being "publishing farmers" ourselves, as we began to develop some ideas for marketing our products with printed matter. Direct oral information was offered to us freely, and it was up to us to sort out the valid advice from the foolishness. Our farming community was seldom willing to review the questions that we brought from our reading.

It was not until we had gardened for a couple of seasons, not until we began selling with other farmers, that I became interested in exploring the agricultural history of our community. Then I began to realize that as a gardener, I was joining the company of millions. And even though I was becoming aware of the fascination that people have always had for growing things, I was in no way prepared for the way in which gardening would become such an obsessive interest. The more we worked in the soil, the more we wanted time for the same. The more we read, the more books we wanted. Our conversations turned with increasing frequency to agricultural topics. We began to visit other farms in the state. We started going to meetings and seminars offered by the extension service or by the Department of Soil Conservation. We began to attend the annual agricultural trade shows in Maine and in the rest of New England. We put ourselves on the mailing lists of any agencies or companies that produced relevant publications.

As we became more familiar with the people and issues involved with agriculture, we began to notice that slight tensions existed between those farmers who used conventional techniques and those who farmed organically. But in our case, the choice to farm without chemicals was less a political statement than the outgrowth of the way we backed into farming for a living. Our first garden, under the Allens' guidance, had been planted for ourselves, our families, and our friends. We hadn't needed to use chemical herbicides or pesticides. When we were first confronted with the choice of whether to combat diseases with chemicals, we felt that we didn't want our own food to be sprayed. We were quite willing to sacrifice some crops, if necessary, for the advantage of having unadulterated food. Once we began to sell food to the public, it wasn't possible, logistically or philosophically, to spray part of the crops for someone we didn't know and leave the rest of it clean for ourselves. There was never any question about our methods. Nor was there the full realization in the early years that our decision to farm without chemicals would affect our choice of crops, of land use, and of marketing strategies. In the early seventies, we were moving ahead much more simply.

Now that we were spending so much time in Maine, we began to look a bit more critically at the farmhouse itself. Initially both of us were quite satisfied with its condition. It was superficially livable, and whatever changes I might have considered had more to do with cosmetic painting and papering than with any basic structural changes. When we started to take a closer look, we realized that we had more substantial problems to contend with. In the basement, we had to replace a few sills and correct some of the foundation stonework. Each of the three chimneys turned out to be unlined, the bricks were cracking, and the masonry was crumbled or loose. The water from the bathroom and kitchen sinks simply ran through a rubber hose and emptied out of the side of the building onto the back lawn. The septic system was unsafe and threatened to contaminate the drinking well at any time.

If we had had the wit to understand how much work would be involved in putting our house back into shape, we would have been overwhelmed. But we realized the problems little by little, and the work was undertaken over a period of several years. We worked on the house mostly during the late fall and winter weekends. In the process, we undertook our first attempts at carpentry, our first work with bricks and mortar, plumbing and wiring. Mark and I were both fortunate to have come from families who had done considerable amounts of work of this kind, so even though we did not have the skills or the vocabulary of the different trades, we were not intimidated by the things we would need to learn. We bought new and used tools from hardware stores or country auctions. We borrowed from our families and neighbors.

Repairing sills and foundations has got to be the most unsatisfying work that we did. All it left us with was the knowledge that the house stood more solidly on its base, but there was nothing to show for the hours of straining and grunting. Tearing down the chimneys was more gratifying, and the job left us with thousands of old bricks that I used to design walkways around the farmhouse. We replaced one of the single-flue chimneys with a double chimney, for a fireplace on one side and a stove on the other. It was a complicated project, so once Mark and I had built the footing for the whole structure, we hired an experienced mason, who agreed to take Mark on as his helper. That way, one of us was able to apprentice, so that in the future we would be able to do our own simple masonry. We learned a lot of tricks from the mason about estimating materials, mixing mortar, breaking bricks accurately, grouting, pointing up. Like all the other things we were undertaking, the first step was acquiring the vocabulary.

In the fall of 1973, with the crops harvested, we turned our weekend attention to the construction of a root cellar and an addition to the back of the farmhouse. We hired a backhoe to dig the space for the foundation, which would measure sixteen by twenty by eight feet deep. We calculated how many cement blocks we would need and how much masonry cement and sand the job would take, and had the supplies delivered. Laying the foundation took all our free time from late October to early December. Mark did most of the work with a friend who was staying at the farm. As the courses of cement blocks increased, the weather grew increasingly cold and stormy. We centered a big old fifty-gallon drum in the work area and kept a small fire going, so that there was at least one spot to warm your body and hands.

On one of the especially dark and raw workdays, I remember, I gathered the speakers of our stereo and placed them close to the work area, thinking that music would ease the chore. Since I was warm and busy inside the farmhouse, I didn't think about the effect of the music on the mood of the workers, and I chose some Buxtehude organ music. It didn't take long for the laborers in the pit to call out that the glories of the Baroque organ did not resound well in a cold, eight-foot-deep hole. The next musical offering was something quite a bit lighter.

The root cellar was finished and boarded over just before the snows came that winter. We left the floor uncemented and ran a small duct from the main heating system, located some twenty-five feet away in the front of the farmhouse. With the small amount of heat that traveled to the root cellar, the temperatures never dipped below thirty-five to forty degrees, even during the coldest winter months. It became a good place to store our root crops: potatoes, carrots, beets, and turnips. Apples kept for months in the cellar, as did our winter storage cabbages, which we harvested by pulling them, roots and all, from the ground and then hung from hooks in the cellar's ceiling. The outer leaves of the cabbages dry out after a few weeks, encasing the inner leaves of the heads. This way we always have fresh cabbage to use for months after their harvest.

We also used the cellar to overwinter our gladiolus bulbs and dahlia tubers in large plastic bags filled with peat moss. The nicest surprise was the success we had with saving our geraniums, right in their pots, where they were allowed to die down and go dormant for the winter. In early spring we brought the pots up into the farmhouse, trimmed back the dead tops, watered the rather stubby-looking plants, and set them in a warm, sunny place. Year after year, the majority of the plants would survive, start sprouting new growth, and be ready to set outdoors with flowers already in blossom. It was such a small effort that I began to wonder why gardeners left their plants out to freeze and die each fall.

Little by little during the next three years we built a room over the cellar, trying to design it so that it blended into the architecture of the existing farmhouse. We started by going to Mark's father, a design engineer in Boston, to help us draw up plans for the addition. Aleksander not only gave us advice on how to build the addition, he gave us a wonderful present — architectural drawings of our whole homestead. Using his plans, we studded the room with strong timbers and roof joists to carry the heavy loads of Maine snow. In retrospect, I realize that we overbuilt the addition, and we took quite a bit of ribbing from our neighbors, who used minimal studding for sheds and sap houses. Aleksander was more accustomed to designing petrochemical plants than small farmhouse additions, but I will say one thing for the addition: it will be standing long after the rest of the farmhouse has grown weary.

Once the basic framing was done, we searched around the Boston contractors' supply houses to find the least expensive six-over-six wooden windows to match those in the other parts of the building. When the room was finished, we were more than a little proud of our work. It blended nicely into the shape of the farmhouse.

We now refer to our addition as the summer room, because we close it off when the weather turns cold in late October. But from mid-April until that time, it is the gathering place for family and friends and people who work with us. The room is dominated by a big old oak table that has lots of extra leaves to accommodate however many of us there are at mealtimes.

It is interesting to reflect on the skills that we were teaching ourselves in the country, because they point out the polarity that was developing between our urban and our rural lives. In the city we bought nearly every service. If something happened to the plumbing, we called the building superintendent. If our car began to cough, we took it to a mechanic. If we wanted houseplants, we bought them in full bloom from a greenhouse. In the country we were beginning to do most things for ourselves, either because the services were not easily available or because they were too expensive for us to consider.

In fact, one of the most significant things that we decided to do for ourselves, the winter after our second vegetable garden, was to attempt to grow our own seedlings. As usual, we went out and bought a few books and sent away for some publications. One of these books became our bible, and I would still recommend it highly to beginners or experienced gardeners. It is called *The Complete Book of Growing Plants from Seed*, by Elda Haring. Haring states early on that she is not a botanist but an enthusiast. She has, however, done her homework, and the book not only provides good basic information about what seeds are and how they perform, it also offers encouragement to novice growers. Over and over, the author points out that this or that works for her, but that every gardener should trust his or her own observations and experiences and use them to enrich conventional wisdom. This spoke directly to the attitudes that I was beginning to develop.

Our first greenhouse, if you can call it that, was so primitive and ill-equipped that it is a wonder anything survived. In fact, it was set up in one of the farmhouse's second-floor bedrooms. The room was on the south side of the house, so it received a modest amount of warmth and light from its one window. We emptied the room entirely of its furniture and filled it up again with plant tables fashioned out of four-by-eight plywood sheets that we turned into shallow trays by nailing boards perpendicular to all four sides. Then we covered the trays with sheets of heavy plastic so that we could water the plants in them. We ordered seeds of every description that winter, figuring that we could experiment freely and not have to buy all our seedlings from a commercial greenhouse next spring.

With the Haring book always handy, we made our own soil mixes and seeded about fifty flats of vegetables, herbs, and flowers. We drenched everything with water and left the flats sitting in about two inches of water in the homemade plywood trays during the weekdays, when we were away at work.

The first weekend after seeding, I think, nothing had germinated, undoubtedly because the farmhouse was heated only to fifty-five degrees on the days we were away. But by the second weekend there were dozens of tiny little cotyledons poking their heads above the soil. This time we had labeled our plants, so we knew what was supposed to be growing in the soil. Nonetheless, we confirmed our labels by comparing the early growth with the illustrations on the endpapers of the Haring book. Yes, our tag said "lupin" and the true leaves looked just like the drawing. And yes, those were marigolds and California poppies, and that was basil. But no, that flat had a couple of different leaf shapes, and only two of them looked like the illustration for cosmos.

About four weeks into our experiment, the plants were beginning to look rather leggy, so we had to rig up artificial lights to compensate for the room's natural darkness. We made a trip to our favorite wrecking company south of Boston and rummaged around until we found some old industrial fixtures. We also found a supply of used fluorescent tubes and mixed those with a few new growing lights. We suspended the lights above each of the seedling trays and set them on automatic timers, so that the plants would benefit not only from more light but from a longer growing day. Watering was as awkward as the rest of the setup, because there was no plumbing on the second floor and we had to carry hundreds of gallons upstairs to our plants.

It's projects like this one that make you appreciate the phrase "beginner's luck." Knowing what I do now about the fickleness of greenhouse plants, I wonder that anything survived the con-

ditions we provided. When it came time to transplant the seedlings, we had hundreds of young plants in varying stages of vigor
and legginess. The undertaking was so simple; our "flats" were
made up of leftover coffee cans, egg cartons, and aluminum baking trays. The look of the room, however, was irrelevant. What
mattered was that we did grow some good plants, and we were
encouraged to continue.

We had watched the Allens harden off their commercially grown
seedlings, and we understood the need to help the plants go from
the protected climate of our farmhouse to the stress of temperature changes, sun, and wind in the fields. So next we built our
first outside greenhouse, which was even more primitive than
the one inside. It consisted of a four-foot-high A-frame covered
with plastic. You had to crawl in and out of the thing, which we
set up on the south lawn. At first we put the plants outside only
during the days, but as the weather grew milder we began to
leave them outside. During the weekdays, my parents or a neighbor would drive over to the farm and water the plants, and if the
nights threatened to turn very cold, someone would throw several
blankets over the outdoor shelter.

I remember being so pleased with our results that I offered to
provide the Allens with some seedlings. They politely accepted
some marigolds. There was no way that they were going to trust
their income crops to our experiments. I remember feeling a bit
insulted at the time, but when farming provided my major income some years later, I revised my thinking.

If I try to evaluate our earliest years at the farm, I realize that
we undertook projects in area after area in which we had little
or no experience. In each case, however, people were available
as teachers, and there was abundant information that we could
borrow, buy, or simply ask to have. We ventured into new territory and our ignorance seldom threatened us, probably because
we were buffered by the confidence we had in our urban capabilities. And the satisfactions of learning always reinforced our
eagerness to move ahead.

It is fair to say that we take on new projects now in fairly deliberate and aggressive ways, but that whole approach is based on some early achievements in all areas of rural living. Each of the skills was significant, but the most important lesson was our growing willingness to rely on ourselves. It is also pertinent to remember that very little of what we were doing was new in the specific sense. All the plants that we raised as crops had been cultivated for years, if not for centuries. All of the carpentry that we were doing was based on some fairly ancient and standard architectural formulas. The attempts that we later made to construct energy-efficient structures were undertaken only after hours of research into the literature that had been produced over the past two decades. If we challenged or modified existing ideas, we did so only after we had made enough mistakes or observations to adjust our plans.

Over the years we have added more basic skills to our inventory, like working on machinery, welding, and learning how to use a computer. There are few mysteries in the skills we have needed to acquire. We recognize what we need to study when we are struggling from lack of information or ability. And I can now say that probably we are less worried about what we do not know than intrigued by the process of having so many new things to learn, so much new information to gather. The development of these attitudes has become the source of our continuing enthusiasm for life in the country.

4 · NOTES ON A DOUBLE LIFE

FROM 1973 UNTIL 1978, Mark and I continued to juggle our professional careers in Boston with what I now think of as our farming apprenticeship in Maine. Initially, it did not occur to either of us that we would want to give up one for the other. They were so different that each served as a vantage point from which we looked at the other with affection and amusement. Our weekdays were peopled with colleagues in publishing and academia, and our weekends were peopled with colleagues who were laborers and vendors.

From early spring until late fall, our Maine work was increasingly dominated by our involvement with the farmers' markets, first in Lewiston, but eventually throughout the state. The first group of Lewiston sellers adopted as its name the Androscoggin Farmers' Market, and after a couple of years of sponsoring only one location, we expanded with two more marketing sites. The first was in Auburn, Lewiston's twin city, and the second was in Rumford, another Maine mill town, located about twenty miles northwest of our farm. Mark and I also joined a farmers' association that organized a different membership nearer the Portland area.

During these years, farmers' markets were developing not just in Maine but all over the country. They were springing up in small rural pockets, sometimes with the support of federal funding, sometimes through the efforts of the national organic farming movement. Markets also began to make their appearance in large cities, as chronicled by John McPhee in a 1978 *New Yorker* article on the first green market in New York City. The similarities between the large urban markets and the small rural ones could not be missed. Full-time farmers, part-time farmers, and backyard gardeners were given the opportunity to bring their fresh produce into towns and cities, to set up instant stores on makeshift tables or on the tailgates of their trucks, and to sell the best portion of a day's pick to enthusiastic consumers. It was a simple idea, with a timely political appeal.

Coming in the early seventies, the markets coincided neatly with the needs of those cities, large and small, that were witnessing the decline of their original downtown commercial sections. With the growth of suburban malls, large numbers of shoppers had been drawn away from inner cities. As a result, merchants' associations and chambers of commerce were working to try to stimulate activity once again in the old downtown sections. In Lewiston, Auburn, and Rumford, the farmers were welcomed by the business community, given free space for selling, and even provided with some financial support for advertising and insurance. In Portland, however, the market did not locate in the downtown section, because an outdoor produce market was already there. This market was like the one that McPhee described, made up of a combination of real farmers and food retailers who simply bought and resold produce that might have been grown anywhere in the world, depending on the season. The newly created Portland group that we joined, made up exclusively of working farmers, chose not to compete with this market, but to accept an offer made by a large Portland shopping mall that had no supermarket on its site. The mall developers were looking for marketing ideas and thought that an outdoor farmers' market would be an attraction, so we were given physical space, along with some advertising support in the mall's media campaigns.

During this same period, many agricultural colleges throughout the country were beginning to assist farmers with marketing strategies, and agricultural extension personnel were often available to help markets organize. Some extension agents were more aggressive and more effective than others, but in nearly every county in Maine at least some attention was given to helping farmers set up direct marketing groups. We were able to use the county extension agency's offices for meetings, and agency staff distributed information and meeting minutes. We had the use of phones and the franking privileges of a government office, which allowed us to do organizing work without the ordinary financial burdens. The coordinating function and the simple availability of space, money, and sympathetic staff people were invaluable in the early years. If it weren't for this support, it is unlikely that many of the individual farmers would have been drawn into such cooperative attempts.

Both Mark and I found our participation in farmers' markets a real adventure. Each of us had had some experience with political activities in college and in the civil rights and war protests of the sixties. By comparison, the organizing of farmers' markets seemed infinitely more manageable. The markets were naturally appealing to sellers and buyers, and the first stages of getting them going were not complex.

But working with farmers' markets was an education in a number of areas that Mark and I had heretofore not appreciated. We needed to learn quickly how to grow new and different crops. We needed to think about the presentation of these products to consumers, about what equipment we needed to own or hire, and about what efforts we would have to make to cultivate a group of customers. On a different but equally important level was the whole question of how a number of independent farmers would come together to structure an organization to serve their needs. Farmers in the various markets came from a variety of backgrounds, but common to most was a fierce independence derived from working their land and marketing their products individually. Cooperative efforts were little understood, and a farmers' market was in part a cooperative, in that it relied on the collective effort of everyone. But at the same time, the market was made up of individuals who would be competing against one another on market day for a limited number of customers. Although there was never any disagreement among members about the wish to make the market successful, there was little agreement over ways to define methods and objectives that everyone could support.

The earliest stages of organizing were the least problematic. The Maine farmers' markets were generally open to anyone who actually grew or produced his or her own products — fruits, vegetables, flowers, herbs, or meat or dairy products. Some of the early markets also included craftspeople, but the mix was not a natural one, and the subsequent growth of craft markets eventually absorbed the various potters, basketmakers, and others who wanted to reach specific audiences. The markets usually formed around a population center and drew on farms within reasonable driving distance of it; on average, participants in the Maine markets traveled between five and fifty miles for a good location. As I have mentioned, the markets were often initiated by extension agencies, but as soon as there were visible models, they began to form when one or two farmers called on some neighbors and a few agreed to meet to sell goods in an available parking lot. It usually took at least one season of selling before the members of any group got together to define their identity, their rules, and their goals.

Those of us who participated in the Androscoggin Farmers'

Market gathered for a potluck supper late in the fall of our first season. Without the tensions of trying to set up and sell, one next to the other, we were able to reflect on that first year with some humor and with critical recommendations for the next season. We decided to form an association with a simple set of bylaws and a slate of officers. The bylaws defined the terms of membership, and as Mark and I worked with other groups in drawing up these terms, we began to see some common ideas. In nearly every market that I became familiar with, members were required to produce most if not all of the items that they sold, and whatever they purchased for resale had to be Maine-grown. Many cities, including Portland and Boston and New York, already had so-called farmers' markets that were really collections of retailers who purchased their produce from food wholesalers. The food might have been grown anywhere in the United States, or even outside the country. The newly forming farmers' markets wanted to distinguish themselves from these food vendors.

At the first organizational meetings, members discussed and agreed on sites and times for selling, and specified market hours. We also had to decide on how many members any given site could support — a decision that required each of us to assess the potential for any market, not so much in actual space but in customers and growth. It was around this issue that some of the first difficulties presented themselves. There was always considerable talk about how "the pie is only so big, and if we invite or allow too many members, then we'll go home with a truckful of leftover produce." Suggestions as to how to make the markets attractive to larger audiences were not well received, nor were suggestions about how markets could attract increasingly larger numbers of sellers and buyers. It seemed that the members were unwilling or unable to imagine that a group effort could generate more success than each of the members had previously experienced as an individual. No one talked about the whole being worth more than the sum of its parts.

If I were to characterize the prevailing attitude of these meetings, I would have to say that it was made up of timidity and fearfulness. We could communicate as a group about the difficulties of raising crops; we could moan about how unappreciative of our fresh produce the customers were, and how city officials and merchants became less and less responsive over the years to our need for more space or assistance. There was an endless list of complaints, and the conversations reflected the lowest sense of collective self-esteem that I had ever witnessed. Visions were limited, and the imagination of the group was rather poor. The critically important subjects of promotion and marketing could not even be kept alive for discussion at meetings. These were areas in which individual members had little experience and no working vocabulary. Mark and I brought to the meetings some concerns and attitudes formed by our earlier political experiences, and a certain outspokenness that was particularly urban. Our aggressiveness offended some, and it is not surprising that many other members of the groups were reluctant to become engaged in the sort of discussions that I would have liked to have had.

A farmers' market was, as I saw it, a real opportunity to attract large numbers of supporters. We had the uniqueness of our physical market. We offered unusual quality and freshness in our produce. We could build the support of community members because each of us was a small business located just at the outskirts of the town or city. Each of us could tell stories about our farms, our products, that would appeal to our customers. As a market, we had the task to inform our customers of our specialness, so that they would be willing to make the extra effort to do part of their shopping outside their customary supermarkets. But each time I or someone else tried to initiate a discussion about the ways in which we could promote our market, most of the other members became impatient or just silent. We were never able to create a dialogue of ideas, or a discussion of individual and group goals.

In addition, market members held conflicting opinions about product pricing and grading, and this was the source of considerable tension as the group continued to come together over a period of several seasons. Some members believed that they needed to compete only in the area of pricing. Some members were careless about grading, and they occasionally held their produce over from one market to the next. They refused to accept the notion that the credibility of the entire market was affected by the behavior of each individual. Some members had not adopted firm policies for their farms, and depending on the pressures they felt at any given market, their tactics would change. A few felt that the members should offer only quality products to the public at all times, and that price wars were not an acceptable approach; instead, these members relied on presentation, quality, reliability, and customer education to sell their products.

I mention a few of the more relevant questions both because they were germane to the growth and development of the cooperatives and, more important, because they are the considerations behind any business. Even in the abstract, they were interesting problems that neither Mark nor I had ever addressed. Each of these questions required a kind of analytical thinking, a demand that we look critically at short- and long-range goals and at the relationship of work to its return at whatever lofty or practical level we wanted to consider. Working with other market members presented us with a series of problems that was intriguing in its complexity.

It seems very neat to list the ideas that came from our participation in farmers' markets and to conclude that they form the basis for our business as it exists today, but it is not overstatement to say that the markets were a good training ground. They were an immediate solution to selling our produce during our first farming years. They were a forum for some shared concerns and a source of information about plants and machinery, and in these nonsensitive areas many of the members were forthcoming with help and advice. The early years of selling gave us the time we needed to improve our land, to learn more about crops, and to gather data that we could use in developing a plan for making a livelihood from our land. Growing for specific markets was a limited demand that we could fit into our schedule. And despite the differences that arose among members of the group, we were deeply bound to one another by a shared appreciation for hard work and a real love for the land.

On the best days, the farmers' markets had all the charm of a small country fair. These days usually came in the late summer, when the morning air was crisp and plenty of buyers were lining up for the boxes of fresh produce. As the day wore on, the temperatures would climb gradually into the high seventies or low eighties and the selling would slow down, so the afternoons became more social than commercial. Over the years, any given market would see an increase in steady customers, each of whom came to talk with one or two farmers, from whom they would do most of their purchasing and to whom they would bring stories of family activities and backyard gardening problems. Some customers would save us their grocery bags or piles of newspapers so that we could recycle them. A few even brought favorite recipes and occasional boxes of old family canning jars, which most of us continued to put to good use on our farms. Anyone who spent any time selling directly in farmers' markets inevitably became addicted to one or another aspect of the market, beyond its ability to provide us with a rather steady income from the middle of July until the end of October.

One aspect that most attracted me was the opportunity to watch people use various expressions for buying and selling and develop varying styles of negotiation. Each of the farms did develop a style, or lack of style, in presenting itself. On the days when selling was good, the level of energy and conversation in the crowd was contagious. On days when produce was just beginning to be plentiful, or when there was a glut of some of the more common items, the markets could take on a mean air. Sellers' faces and gestures betrayed their anxiety about taking

home quantities of unsold food. There were often caustic exchanges between farmers over individual decisions to drop prices,
to give way to fear and, as we would say, "give the stuff away
rather than bring it home to the pigs or the compost piles."
Sometimes there were open hostilities between buyers and sellers, when someone tried to bargain over a price. Some farmers
were openly willing to haggle, whereas others were clearly offended by the suggestion.

During the last months of any selling season, the mornings
grew increasingly cold, and setting up the trucks was a real chore.
If there were rains in addition to the cold, as there are so often
in the late summer and early fall, then the crowds of shoppers
would thin out. Late in the season, we were all overextended on
our farms, trying hard to gather in the last produce before the
heavy frosts and to haul in enough wood to dry a few cords before
the really cold weather came. Tempers were usually short at
some of the last market days, when farmers felt less in control
of their sales and less certain of their income, much of which
had to be saved and meted out for living expenses during the
winter and early spring months, when there was little beyond
wood, animal products, and maple syrup to bring in cash.

But despite the more pessimistic moods of the markets, their
constantly changing personality and vitality remained fascinating. Even when Mark and I had little to sell, or when we had just
finished a particularly difficult week of work in Boston, neither
of us would have considered missing a day of selling.

Our first store-on-wheels was an old half-ton Chevy pickup,
with a tired body of dark green mixed with several areas of rust.
We outfitted the platform with a homemade cap built from two-
by-fours and some sheets of plywood, which we painted to match
the truck (the green part, that is). We built movable shelves on
the inside to store our produce, and over the seasons we modified
the inside to accommodate just as much harvest as the half-ton
springs would support. The types and varieties of truck modifi-
cations that farmers came up with would make a fascinating
visual study. Some people were extremely clever in converting

a van or a pickup into a movable store. As the markets developed
in strength and number across the state, the competition in truck
design became more evident.

The skills you needed in our category of direct marketing were
quite straightforward. You planted, cultivated, and then harvested and packed a truck as full as possible with as great a variety
of produce as you could manage. Then you got in your truck at
first light and headed out carefully over bumpy country roads,
trying to avoid the roughest spots so you could get your produce
safely to the market. Assuming that you didn't have a flat tire,
a broken heater hose, or goods blowing out of the back of the
vehicle, you arrived at the market in time to unload hundreds
and hundreds of pounds of merchandise as quickly as possible.
Then you tried to arrange everything into an appealing display
while the inevitable handful of before-opening-hour shoppers were
rifling through your best produce, handling it in ways that would
have got your field hands fired. They were also peppering you
with questions about the price of each and every item, long before
you had had a chance to make the decisions, let alone letter the
price cards that had to be affixed to each of the containers on the
display table. Then you had to set up the scales, which had not
yet been inspected by the city inspector, who was, as it happened,
rounding the corner at this very moment, with his briefcase of
standard weights and seals in hand. The cash box, which you
thought your partner had put in the front seat of the truck, had
been left at the farm, and so you rummaged around through your
jacket and pants pockets to pull together enough change to get
you through the first couple of sales. Your first customer inevitably handed you a twenty, and you had to rush to the farmer
next to you and beg some change so that you could finish the
sale. Having collected yourself — because the first sales have a
way of reassuring even the seasoned vendor that the day will not
be a total failure — you relaxed into a mode that you hoped would
attract, cajole, and entertain prospective buyers into purchasing
as many of your goods as possible by the end of the market.

When the most hectic hours of selling were over, you looked

at what hadn't sold and tried to rearrange it in different containers. Perhaps the radishes would do better next to the vegetable marrows. Someone should have put the Brussels sprouts into a smaller container and placed them next to the turnips, because they didn't look appealing between the green cukes and green beans. As you were doing that, you asked yourself how many more times you could answer, "That's an eggplant. It's very popular in Greek and Italian cooking, and . . ." before the questioner would frown and walk on. Then, as the shoppers thinned out and disappeared altogether, you began to pack up the leftover produce, the boards, tables, bricks, and endless paraphernalia of the store, and returned to the farm, with as many empty boxes as possible and enough money to satisfy yourself that the time and effort had been justified.

For those of us who continued with this for any period of time — and the enormous effort involved caused many to drop out in the first few years — there was a fascination with the process and its potential for success. Also, we felt we could evaluate this method of marketing fairly accurately, and after a year or two in any given market, we began to project the potential for income and the marketability of items. Our first efforts were based on our analysis of the data that I collected in the farm journals and notebooks that I mentioned earlier. These journals, full of years and years of data, gave us a real picture of our undertaking, including information on planting dates, seed varieties and costs, sizes of plantings, times and quantities of harvest, and the fluctuation of consumer demands at the markets.

For instance, on the subject of consumer tastes, my journals remind me of our customers' reluctance to buy fresh peas at the end of the summer. Peas were in demand on the Fourth of July, and none of us could haul enough of them to our customers on or around that date. But those of us who succeeded in producing the lovely Wando heat-resistant varieties that matured in August were often disappointed to see customers pass them by for green and yellow beans. I have also watched as a vendor had a hard time selling everbearing raspberries because they were available for sale at what seemed a non-raspberry time. Supermarket shoppers may flock to the bins of Chilean fruit in February, but at the farmers' markets, our customers had fixed ideas about when to expect and when to eat certain produce. Perhaps this behavior was due to the fact that many of our buyers had not been long off the family farms themselves. (Mark informs me that it is humans' basically conservative eating habits that have insured the survival of the species. That's when he is speaking as an anthropologist. When he was speaking as a farmer selling — or in this case, not selling — his Wando peas in August, he was less theoretical.)

On our way home from each daily market, one of us would drive while the other tallied up the sales for the day. Back at the farm, I usually took all of the notes from that day's sales and organized them into a list including each product's name, the price per pound for that particular day, and the total taken in on each product. With this detailed record keeping, we could appropriate to an individual crop a relative value, based on its cost to raise and harvest and its marketability. But that was only a one-dimensional assessment, and over the first several years of direct marketing, we found that there were many other, equally important factors that affected our ability to sell our produce.

From the beginning, the quality of our vegetables was of extreme importance to both Mark and me, in great part because we were so proud of our newly found ability to grow beautiful produce. We began to grade our crops very strictly, knowing full well that the eye appeal of our vegetables was as important to the consumer as the fact that they were freshly picked and grown without chemicals. In fact, for the first few years of selling, we didn't even advertise that we farmed organically. We had not adopted it as a public position, and we were not trying to make a statement about it. If people asked about our methods, we told them, but our basic aim was to offer the most appealing display of as broad a variety of vegetables as we could grow. We carefully

planned the layout of our items, juxtaposing complementary colors
and shapes in bins that we designed and built out of plywood
and painted a warm brick red. We heeded Clarence's advice, and
our stand became increasingly popular.

Early on in our marketing, we sometimes rented two stall
spaces. Although we were far from the largest farm at the market,
we wanted the display to seem spacious. We knew that in order
to attract customers to our area, we needed to appeal to some
basic impulses — and in this case, we offered an abundant and
visually pleasing choice. The abundant choice meant that we
grew a large variety of crops, well beyond the popular cukes,
tomatoes, beans, and corn. Some of our crops were eggplants,
shell beans, vegetable marrows, horseradish roots, and onions,
which we sold either by the pound or done up in beautiful braids.
Some of these vegetables were costly to raise, but they served
wonderfully as lures to get customers to stop, look, and ask questions. Even if many of these customers ended up buying a pound
of string beans or three cukes for a quarter, we had the advantage
of attracting a large portion of any market crowd to our display.

The mode of interaction that we consciously chose to cultivate
with our customers was one in which we offered information
about the farm or about the food we grew, because that was the
way in which we could most honestly convey our particular
interests in farming. We began by writing and mimeographing
small handouts on food use and preparation, especially for the
less familiar crops. We talked about the nutritional value of foods,
and when we began to offer herbs, we talked about the possibility
of substituting herbs for salt in cooking, something that we had
begun to do when our son was on the way. Since the gathering
of information was our particular orientation in farming, we found
that sharing information was for us the most natural way to sell.

Whatever the business, it seems that the seller has to evaluate
the way in which he or she can reach the audience. Our approach
was one of a number of methods that we observed in the group.
Some farmers held on solidly to the approach of always trying

to have the earliest popular produce. Some always lowered their prices to have the least costly items, and quite a few made no effort to interact with the customers. Sometimes out of shyness, and sometimes out of indifference, farmers and their hired help would sit on the tailgates of their trucks, barely paying attention to the people who passed before their displays.

My earliest selling experiences convinced me that customers are as interested in the kind of exchange that takes place between the buyer and seller as they are in the money or goods being traded. And further, I am certain that the appeal of the farmers' markets was due in part to the fact that consumers once again had the opportunity to purchase from an actual producer. In small towns like the ones in which we were selling, people could remember the pleasures of shopping in stores that were owned by families from their own communities, where the clerks often stayed on as employees for years. When community-owned shops were replaced by the franchises that populate nearly every shopping mall, there was a marked change in the experience of shopping. When we farmers were often back downtown, comments and complaints could once again be passed directly between buyers and sellers.

In deciding what customers we were best suited to cultivate, Mark and I felt that we could not depend on the loyalty of a clientele who shopped for price alone. Those buyers were usually at the market very early in the morning, before the trucks had actually set up, or they showed up regularly when the day was nearly over, looking for farmers who were happy to take any amount of money rather than pack up their unsold products and take them back home. These customers played farmers off against one another, as they scurried from booth to booth, asking the prices and hoping to get a better verbal offer than the posted price. Farmers who tried to court this clientele had to be able to sustain a basically adversarial relationship with a fickle group. I watched over the years and saw how this eroded the pleasures of the market and embittered some sellers and buyers.

In addition, as I am fully aware, my approach to marketing in the mid-seventies was unencumbered by the fear that I wouldn't make enough money to get my family through the upcoming week or year. Our early attitudes about how to develop our business didn't need to be cautious, both because we were not relying on the income and because we were not in any heavy capital debt for land, labor, or machinery. Inversely, the ability to think relatively freely about the development of our farm affected our decisions in the areas of expansion, capital investment, and the definition of an appropriate scale and diversity. Our farming was rooted in our early pleasures of discovery and learning, and to the degree that we continue to evaluate it in those terms and try to make its goals mesh with some economic realities, we are successful.

By the mid-seventies, I was rather firmly rooted in my work as the art director for *The Atlantic Monthly* magazine. In the fall of 1974 our son, Jacob, was born, and at the same time Mark turned away from an early career in photojournalism to begin a graduate program in medical anthropology. When I think back on all those demands on our time and energy, they seem impossible, but at the time we were not willing to give up any of our activities and were willing to work as hard as we had to to sustain all of our interests.

One of the things that helped us lead our double, or perhaps triple, lives was the fact that I had negotiated with the magazine to let me work in the city for four days a week and to do whatever additional work was needed in Maine over the three-day weekend. I could read manuscripts and assign artwork in Maine just as well as in my office in Boston, so revising my schedule seemed quite reasonable. The editor of the magazine did not understand at all why anyone would want to live on a farm in Maine, or why anyone would have the nerve to expect to be given a four-day work week, and my request led to some tense negotiations. I was fully prepared to change my schedule, even if it meant looking elsewhere for design work, but the editor eventually agreed, after he got over the shock of the request. I must also admit that he was perhaps more prescient than I and could foresee my gradual withdrawal from the city.

Mark rearranged his schedule of classwork and teaching at graduate school so that he too could get to Maine for three days every week. If we had been restricted to a traditional five-day work week in one place, the simultaneous development of our farm and our professional lives would not have been possible. Instead, we restructured our time so that we now had a seven-day work week, but the kinds of work that we were doing were so diverse that each was an antidote for the other, both physically and intellectually.

Each place also became an outrageous contradiction of the other. From Friday night until Tuesday morning, I lived and labored in a world of people who worked with their hands and their machines in and out of doors. The men I grew to know best and be fondest of had permanently stained, machine-scarred hands. They wore baseball caps or caps advertising tractors or fertilizer companies. Their blue or green heavy cotton work clothes were threadbare around the collars and cuffs. They wore construction boots summer and winter, always with white socks. They either held strong opinions against smoking or rolled their own cigarettes and were never seen without one hanging out of a corner of the mouth. Their summer tans ended at the edges of their T-shirts, and each season continued to weather skin that didn't have time to bleach out completely during the winter. Conversations with many of these men were usually halting, sometimes downright spare, but almost always uncalculating. Most of them drove around in cars or trucks with odometers on their second or third round.

The women I met at the markets or on neighboring farms all knew how to run a household on a shoestring. I would meet them often when we were shopping at the Salvation Army store, looking for some work clothes for the adults or regular clothes for the kids. Everyone cooked, canned, and froze food from the gardens to last a full year, and nearly every farm raised part or all of its meat. We women all tied our hair back in bandannas or kerchiefs when we were working in the field or selling. Many of us were plump, if not downright overweight. I'm not certain why it always seemed to me that the women looked more tired than the men. I seldom saw what these women did to themselves when they went out on Saturday nights, but whatever personal vanities they possessed seldom got attention on working days.

From Tuesday morning until Friday evening, the scenery was quite different. I spent all of my working hours in an office in one of Boston's lovely old brownstones, facing the Public Garden. No one had stained hands; in fact, I had to spend a few minutes at the end of each weekend trying to repair my own hands with bleach and lemon juice and hand cream, so that I would not feel self-conscious about them in the city. There was a work uniform at the magazine, as there is among any group of people who carefully protect their status and associations by the way in which they present themselves. The publishing business seems to attract individuals who place value on casual good taste and definitely not on conspicuous trendiness, and people at the magazine wore sports coats, suits, ties, sweaters, skirts, blouses, and dresses in the unmistakably conservative Boston tradition. There were definitely no white socks and no bandannas. If the men wore hats, which they did on occasion, they were usually the requisite soft-brimmed Irish wool types. Women had good haircuts, and were seldom plump. It was not uncommon to see an L. L. Bean catalogue on a colleague's desk, but the work clothes that he or she ordered were seldom for working. Smoking was becoming less and less evident, as many of us gave it up and then gently chastised the few diehards to do the same.

Despite the obvious visual differences between my colleagues in these two workplaces, it was their styles of communicating that were the most startlingly different. In Maine, our successes and strengths were hauled out and displayed on the market tables each Saturday. Few felt the need to embellish the physical evidence. In publishing and academia, however, one always feels the need to display oneself verbally. It is the very essence of daily exchange, and each individual's ability to perform well is proof of his or her worth. Style and wittiness could become so in demand that they were applauded for themselves, without regard for the substance of the discussion or ideas. But I must add that the constant juxtaposition of one style with the other kept me amused and stimulated, and I was addicted to both arenas. Each group had little real feeling for or understanding of the other, and each was disdainful of the values and abilities of the other. The members lived in dramatically different economic circumstances, but more important, they functioned in totally different physical environments.

Probably one of the most significant factors in our decision to move to Maine was my increasing dissatisfaction with actually having to live in the city. The more that we worked outdoors at the farm, the more I found it uncomfortable to be confined to an office for many hours each day. I was very pleased with my work at the magazine, and I was deeply attached to a number of my colleagues. But I was coming to find the physical environment oppressive. The longer I lived in the city, the more I came to resent the noise, the congestion, and the anxieties of people in their cars and on the subways. I began to lobby for the move to Maine.

Mark, in contrast to me, was probably more at home in the city than in Maine at that time. He had lived most of his life in cities, first in Russia, then in Poland, and then in this country. He was somewhat receptive to the idea of a move, but was less optimistic than I was about our chances of surviving in the country. There ensued months of discussions, agreements, disagreements, and finally a joint attempt to evaluate what we might be able to do to make a living. We pieced together some rough plans, trying to work out a way to rely on income from our gardening along with income that we might be able to earn from our other professions. By this time we were making about $2500 from our gardens. We imagined that we could surely double, if not triple, that amount if we were living in Maine full-time. And we knew that we would not be able to move for a few years, because Mark had to finish his classwork as a graduate student before he began writing his dissertation. That would give us time to save a bit of money — at least enough to get us through our first year on the farm.

As the months went by and we continued to work, study, and save, Maine continued to be the place we most wanted to live. I was determined that we could make a life there that would nourish us in ways the city could not. Mark and I also felt that it was the richest environment we could offer to Jacob. Our son had spent most of his life in the city, first spending days with a nanny and then in a day-care center. Those were good experiences for him, particularly because they allowed him to have the company of other children; for an only child, that was important. But the sensibilities that a rural life informs, I felt certain, must be experienced firsthand.

There was little about the physical environment of Maine that I did not love. Our farmhouse was spacious and quiet — hauntingly so for many of our urban friends who visited. The land around was a mixture of fields, wetlands, and small mountains. The water from the hand-dug well was clear and plentiful. Every season offered a banquet of pleasures — not verbal ones, as many of my urban pleasures were, but sensual ones.

As our attachments to Maine deepened, Mark and I talked about it less frequently with colleagues in Boston. Maine farm life does not translate well into words. In fact, Mark felt that he had to hide his interest in agriculture from other members of his graduate school department, lest he not be taken seriously as a scholar. In all truthfulness, I too edited my conversations at the magazine, choosing carefully the friends with whom I openly discussed my love of rural life.

The years of preparation went rapidly, and in January 1978 I told the magazine that I would be leaving in three months. And so, in April of that year, we packed the contents of our Beacon Street apartment into the back of a pickup truck and began our journey up the Maine Turnpike, a journey that we had made every Friday evening for the past seven years of our lives. But this time we wouldn't be returning on Tuesday morning.

5 · COMMITMENT

TO THIS DAY, I never hear the Telemann Suite for Flute and Strings without remembering our weekly trips to Boston. At seven o'clock on Tuesday mornings, "Morning Pro Musica" opened on the radio with this theme, and if we were running on schedule, it meant that we should be somewhere on the Maine Turnpike between Auburn and Gray. That would allow us to slip into Boston just after the nine o'clock jam on the Tobin Bridge and arrive at our Beacon Street apartment in time for me to shower, change, and dash to work. In the meantime, Mark would take Jacob to the day-care center and then go to the anthropology department or to one of his classes. That had been our routine for so many weeks, for so many years, that only a few notes of the Telemann piece bring it all back. When we first moved to Maine, I was struck with more than a twinge of anxiety whenever I heard the music. As the years progressed, the anxiety was replaced by a rather smug amusement, and now the memory is distant and sentimental.

In planning our move, we made certain to save a few thousand dollars to cushion the dramatic change in our earning ability for the first year or so. But even more important, I had contracted with a Cambridge-based political magazine, then known as *Working Papers*. For an annual fee of some $12,000, I was to design the bimonthly, working primarily in Maine and traveling six times a year to Boston to do the final work on each issue before it went to the printer. We felt that for a few years, at least, we could manage on a somewhat predictable, if not spare, income.

We are often asked whether we were afraid to take the risk of throwing away all our urban affiliations for the uncertainties of a life in Maine. At the outset, our excitement at the prospect of living full-time at the farm overshadowed whatever doubts we had, and there was very little time to reflect on what we had given up. We were simply too busy trying to work on the house, the gardens, and the wood lots. Furthermore, Mark still had several years of research to do to complete his doctorate, and we had a young son to enjoy without having to leave him for eight or nine hours each day. But there was a lot at stake. Having made a bold statement that we were willing to leave some urban accomplishments behind, we were stubbornly determined to make the change work out, for the sake of our pride if nothing else.

There were many other people heading for the woods in those days, and many of them were leaving graduate programs and professions, just as we had. Some of us were more prepared than others for the realities of homesteading. Regardless of how much we were willing to scale down our consumption, there were still some basic needs that we had to meet: shelter, food, clothing, almost always some form of transportation, basic medical care, and whatever entertainment each of us felt was essential. Any romantic notions many of us had about the simplicity or purity of life in the country were soon countered by the need to provide at least a minimum stable income. Many people exhausted their savings within the first few years and had to look for jobs off their land, and when that happened, their idealized notions of homesteading were modified with some sobering facts of life that almost any indigenous rural person already knew firsthand. We watched as one homesteader after another in our own community looked for work in the surrounding areas. Women found it very difficult to find jobs that paid anything, and many of the men ended up working on carpentry crews. There is a bittersweet joke among many of the transplanted men in our area about having put in time as carpenters, despite backgrounds in journalism, engineering, music, or academia.

Certainly Mark and I did and still do our share of carpentry. The main difference is that we have done it entirely while repairing and building at our own farm as the business has grown. Whatever foresight we had in making plans for some initial economic stability, however small, turned out to be one of the most important things we did. The second key to our survival was probably our emotional preparation for the work we would do here. We were thoroughly familiar with the relentless and often tedious demands of farming, and although we still held some naive notions about the pleasure of working the land, these were countered by the seven years of work we had done before we moved.

We are still not fully unpacked from the move. Boxes of dishes, assorted kitchen gadgets, and books are stored in the attic. Eventually they will make their way to a thrift-store hopper, or be given away for a rummage sale. But we arrived early enough in the year to settle in superficially — the real nesting would be done the following winter — with the work of getting our land ready for the first full-time garden ahead of us. We were so enthusiastic that spring, imagining that we had unlimited time for whatever we wanted to grow. Each day we tackled part of a new plot east of the house, clearing out a small area so we could break in the soil with a crop of potatoes. We designed new perennial beds and plantings around the farmhouse. We created a large lawn on the western slope behind the house and transplanted a couple of small maples, completing the circle of trees around the farmhouse. We ordered seeds of vegetables we had not yet tried, such as soy, lima, kidney, soldier, and pea beans and different varieties of chard, spinach, and eggplant. We began to plant more varieties of herbs. We ordered and set out some two hundred gladiolus bulbs, along with tubers of cactus and standard-blooming dahlias. (The burden of digging, curing, and storing those flowers' corms and tubers haunted us for several years, until we finally agreed that we truly disliked glads and the dahlias were more work than we could handle in the fall.)

The physical labor was endless, exhilarating, and we both watched our bodies grow stronger and actually change in proportion. Carrying, bending, digging, lifting, hoeing, weeding — and my legs, shoulders, and forearms became heavily muscled and strong. In fact, I had never felt in better shape physically, except for my back, which ached at the end of every day. As it turned out, Mark's most vulnerable parts were his feet, and many a night he still comes in from work and fills a pail with warm soapy water to soak them in. I clearly recall collapsing into bed each night, satisfied that we had done so much around the farm and grateful for a good mattress and the deep sleep that follows real physical exertion.

During the next three years, our work, experimentation, and marketing efforts did begin to produce significant increases in the income we were generating from our farm. With only a slight increase in land under cultivation, our gross farm income climbed quickly from less than $3000 in 1977 to a bit over $13,000 in 1980. A great deal of that increase could be attributed to the fact that we were farming full-time, but we were also planting our gardens differently, choosing our crops in different proportions, looking for new markets, and working to promote the visibility of our farm, in the hope that we could gradually wean ourselves from our urban income.

We focused our attention first on plants and growing methods. Since we had begun with so little horticultural knowledge, we had chosen our crops on the advice of other farmers and added to the selection with some whimsical choices of seeds and plants offered through the various seed catalogues. It took years of growing and selling experience before we could begin to make some considered decisions about what to grow and how to grow it. From that experience, I can offer a few observations.

Magazines such as *Horticulture, Pacific Horticulture,* and *Organic Gardening* will provide the beginner with the names and addresses of a number of the better-known seed companies and nurseries. For more involved gardeners, or for those who are searching for specific suppliers, a valuable source book was published in 1986 by Barbara Barton; it is called *Gardening by Mail.* Barton, a former reference librarian, has compiled an extensive list of seed companies and nurseries, garden supply companies, horticultural societies, useful gardening books, horticultural libraries, and horticultural magazines and newsletters.

Seed and plant catalogues make any number of claims for their offerings, including details about earliness and quantity of yield, hardiness, disease resistance, eye appeal, and taste. Seed companies also make varied efforts to comment on how the plants will perform in different geographical locations. As it became increasingly important to us to have reliable crops, we narrowed our choices of catalogues to those that seemed to give thorough horticultural information. There is usually a direct correlation between a company's reliability and the lack of hyperbole it uses in making claims for its products.

Ideally, companies should offer customers the following information:

- Both common and botanical names of the plants. There can be endless confusion if only common names are used, particularly for some trees, shrubs, herbs, and flowers.

- Information on the amount of seeds in a package or the number of seeds in the amount (an ounce, usually) that you will be able to order. You will be amazed to find that well-known companies do not tell you how much you are buying.

- The germination rates of given seeds. You may need only ten seeds of something that has a ninety-percent germination rate, but you will need one hundred seeds of something with a germination rate of nine percent.
- A brief but accurate description of the soil and temperature conditions for optimum germination and growth.
- The approximate number of days from seeding to flower and fruit harvest.
- The hardiness of the plant in different climate zones.
- The resistance of the plant to the most common and difficult diseases or insect pests.

When buying seeds and plants, you are also well advised that many seed companies have both wholesale and retail catalogues, and unless you ask specifically, you will probably be sent the retail one. Not knowing this, we ordered for several years from the retail listings, when in many cases we were ordering amounts large enough to qualify us as wholesale buyers. In addition, there is always the possibility of group purchases, which we sometimes attempted with other members of the farmers' markets. But even if you find that you are purchasing primarily from wholesale catalogues, you might want to study the retail listings as well. The wholesale offerings are usually restricted to the most popular plant species and varieties, and you may find that you want to include more unusual plants in your gardens.

It was not until we had farmed for a number of years that we realized that seed companies function in a number of different ways. There are companies that raise, harvest, cure, and package all of their own seeds. There are companies that have no agricultural facilities or experience, and that purchase all of their seeds from growers throughout the world. In between these two extremes are the majority of companies, which both purchase and produce their vast inventories of seeds and plants. As we have developed special-interest areas at the farm, we have occasionally found it helpful to write or call seed companies to ask whether they can give us additional information from the field tests they have conducted on individual crops. Reputable companies — both small and large — should be willing to answer questions or direct you to sources of further information.

When ordering seeds, you should also know which kinds will keep for a year or two, in case you overorder (a tendency that we are still trying to curb). Some seeds, such as cole crops and onions, can be stored in a cool, dry place, and their germination rate will not decrease much over a period of two to three years. Others, such as beets and parsnips, are not worth storing for even a year after purchase. Since seed prices have risen sharply during the past decade, it is no small economy to purchase carefully. You might also want to consider whether the plants are hybrids or not. If they are, then you will have little or no success in saving your own garden seeds, whereas nonhybrid varieties produce seeds that you can collect and use. We have begun to collect and save increasing amounts of our herb and flower seeds, especially when we find colors and plant qualities that we want to propagate. As our skills with seed collection and storage increase, we are finding that our seeds are often more vigorous than their commercially produced counterparts. Even if you are a weekend gardener, I would encourage you to try collecting some seeds from your own garden for the experience alone. It will press you into looking more closely at your plants when they are at the end of their production cycle, past their visual prime. You might be intrigued by the beauty of seed pods and the fascinating differences in seed shapes, sizes, and yield.

In addition to choosing your seeds and plants from companies you feel are reputable, you may also want to shop around for the best prices, especially if you are ordering hundreds of dollars' worth of seeds and plants each year, as we are now doing. Every first and second week of January, we spread out dozens of catalogues on our kitchen table, list the seeds we need, and compare information and prices. We order from wherever we feel we will get the best quality, price, and reliable delivery. Over the past decade we have seen greater standardization of pricing in the seed and plant industry, but there are still enough inconsistencies to make shopping around worthwhile. When purchasing seeds for the crops from which we expect large cash yields, we take yet another precaution, by ordering seeds from several suppliers so we have some insurance in the event of a crop failure or mishandling of seeds. This can save a lot of money and anguish. For instance, I spoke recently with a commercial flower grower from Indiana who had ordered a specific color of *Limonium*, or statice as it is commonly known, from a reliable company, and the crop turned out to be a different color — a color that was particularly unmarketable. Similarly, one year when we were counting on every penny from our vegetable garden, we ended up with 150 hills of yellow pattypan squash where we thought we had sown blue Hubbard. When this happens — and it is not infrequent — the seed company usually issues an apology and replaces the seed at no cost, but that does little to offset losses for a commercial grower.

We used seeds carelessly in our first gardens. We often threw handfuls along a furrow, or dropped them into place with the corn and bean planter. If the seeds were planted too closely, then we had to thin the rows by hand. If they were too far apart, we would reseed, time permitting, or cultivate the space to prevent large weeds. There was no predictable relation between seed use and yield from one year to the next.

Also, we had been taught to plant crops in long, narrow, ribbonlike rows, with enough space between each row to drive a horse, tractor, or tiller. That meant that the proportion of vegetative cover to work space in a given acre was heavily weighted in favor of uncultivated space. We have since learned that many crops are best planted in wide rows, and once you rethink a garden with this design, you immediately change the productive area and greatly reduce the spaces to be cultivated. We have probably experimented with every permutation that one can imagine in laying out our gardens, and as of this writing, we have settled on a method that results in the highest yields of first-quality produce.

All of the rows in our annual gardens and most in our perennial gardens are planted on raised beds, which we shape with the hillers of the tractor and then manually smooth over with iron rakes. (The job of smoothing could be done with the tractor too, if we fashioned a rake to be hauled on the work bar of the machine, so that the hillers pile up the soil and the rake follows.) We thus have a series of rows two to three feet wide by perhaps six to eight inches high, each about 450 feet long in the largest, main garden. We then cover the raised rows with four-foot-wide black plastic mulch. You can get machines that lay plastic mulch, but having worked both ways, we have chosen to do our mulching by hand. This means that two people actually carry and stretch the rolls of plastic over the raised beds, while a third hoes dirt into piles every five or six feet along both edges. When the row is covered, someone drives over it with the tractor, keeping the wheels of the machine just outside the plastic and steering the potato hillers so they draw soil in to bury the edges of the plastic completely. Any loose edges of plastic can be caught by the wind and torn free from the fields. It is also important to draw the plastic tightly over the width of the row, so the wind cannot reach down through the planting holes and turn your whole raised row into a giant sail.

You do not have to coordinate the mulching of the field with the planting, but you do need to get all of the plastic mulch down early, when the soil is still moist. We made the mistake of putting down plastic over a dry section of the field one year, and had to contend with a desert under the mulch and with plants that struggled all summer simply to survive.

As soon as the plastic is laid over the raised rows, we cover the walkways between the rows, first with several layers of paper and then with a hay mulch. This allows the rain to penetrate the field at the same time that it suppresses weeds. The paper- and hay-covered walkways also provide a clean and comfortable path for general maintenance and harvesting. When we began using this kind of cover, we bought and used discarded newspaper from the local dump. It did the job, but it was tedious and sometimes difficult to put down, especially if it was windy. Trying to solve that problem led us to use the butt ends of printing paper — leftover rolls of paper from large printing presses, such as those that print magazines and newspapers. They are usually available at little or no cost from area printers, who typically have to dispose of them anyway. We found a printer who was actually delighted to see the paper put to some good use. He had built his company with the same frugality that causes Mark and me to fabricate and scrounge whenever possible.

It has taken us more than a dozen years to get to this method of planting, and during that time we have attempted to plant and cultivate with tractors, tillers, and hours of hoeing. Since we chose to farm organically, we built up our soil over the years with tons of animal manure, lime, and compost. In the process, we created a wonderful place not only for crops but for luxurious amounts of pigweed, galinsoga, chickweed, and amaranth, some of which came to us with the animal manure. We tried to cultivate the gardens each year, before we used our mulching technique, and inevitably lost ground with one or another crop, usually the small-seeded kinds such as carrots, beets, dill, and onions. We simply could not keep up with the weeds.

When we first started using the complete mulching system, we assumed that we could set into the plastic only the more traditional transplants such as tomatoes, peppers, cole crops, and the like. Now we put almost no seeds directly into our gardens. Everything is set out as transplants, including beets, onions, peas, beans, turnips, chard, dill, chamomile, cucumbers, squashes, and gourds. We jokingly refer to our fields as our instant gardens, because immediately after planting they are a tapestry of vegetables, herbs, and flowers, all set out as young, hardened-off plants. The results have been impressive.

During March, April, and May, we sow specific numbers of

these crops in the greenhouses or cold frames, timing them so that the transplants are ready to go into the field whenever the nighttime temperatures permit. We transplant our field seedlings into large commercial plugs, fifty plugs to a tray. This allows each plant to develop in its own cell, and when we transplant from the plugs to the ground, the individual root balls are not disturbed. Regardless of the vagaries of the spring weather, the seeds are germinated and grown to a specific stage under controlled conditions.

We harden off the seedlings and always wait for a cloudy day or a series of rainy days to transplant into the field. Depending on the size of the plant, we make a hole in the plastic over each raised row just large enough to work through. Ideally, the plastic should fit snugly around the stem of the plant, but we have to provide working space for our fingers and enough room for the root ball of the seedling. We work carefully not to rip the plastic, because anyplace where sunlight and water come into contact with bare soil is ground in which weed seeds can germinate. About two to three weeks after the young seedlings are set out, we have to go over each and every row, replacing the few plants that have been destroyed by cutworms, wind, mice, or insects. We also have to pick out whatever weeds there are. But after that first repairing, the seedlings are usually large enough to crowd out any further weed growth, and they are generally strong enough to withstand weather fluctuations and other stresses.

Although the labor of mulching and planting is uncommonly demanding in the early part of the season, we have found that we use less seed, have a very high ratio of plants that live to harvest, and are freed from the overwhelming tedium of maintenance and the frustration of giving up parts of our gardens to weeds. Hardy transplants also show a greater tolerance of stresses in weather and early insect damage. In some ways, this method is simply a reallocation of labor: we spend more time with young plants in the greenhouses than in the fields, and planting is usually a several-week rather than a several-day operation. But once we have finished these tasks, we have eliminated the weeks and weeks of labor that we initially spent on weeding, thinning, and constant cultivation.

We have tried several times to experiment with direct seeding in the plastic-covered rows, by making small holes and seeding where we want the plants to emerge. The results have been un-even. Our potatoes responded very well. We used a bulb planter with a long handle to cut deep holes into the raised rows, and then dropped cut-up pieces of seed potatoes into the holes and filled them with dirt. The plants sprouted quickly in the warm, moist soil, and the potatoes never needed the weeding and hilling that our traditionally planted acreage had required. We had less success with some beans that we seeded into holes in the mulch. Some young cotyledons appeared, but a large number either dried out or rotted because of uneven soil conditions or the lack of good air circulation just beneath the plastic. We need to repeat these efforts several more seasons before I can rule out their chances for success. We also need to find a way to grow carrots in plastic-covered beds, because they can become quite mis-shapen when transplanted.

Despite these few problems with the method, I find that it is practicable for both large-scale commercial operations and back-yard gardening, particularly for those whose working schedules keep them from cultivating their gardens as frequently as they should. I've talked with many people who say that they gave up their kitchen gardens because they didn't want to use sprays and they simply could not keep up with the weeding.

My main objection to the whole process really rests on the wide-scale use of black plastic, both because it is aesthetically unpleasing and because it is not a recyclable material. But I think that we are a short time away from the development of a plant-based mulch that will do the same work as the plastic, and we will be able to disc that back into the soil as a beneficial additive. I read just recently that a patent is being sought for a biodegrad-able mulch that looks and behaves like black plastic but that is made from a corn starch. Whether or not this discovery becomes a manufactured and affordable item really depends on our attitudes as consumers. Needless to say, I am hoping for its success.

The evolution of our seeding and planting techniques was paralleled by our experimentation with a variety of greenhouses and cold frames, starting with the primitive arrangements that I described earlier. Just before leaving Boston, we decided to give ourselves a last luxurious present, knowing that for a number of years we would not be able to indulge ourselves as consumers. We looked at the various greenhouses that were then on the market. We were primarily interested in glass and aluminum structures that could be permanently attached to the farmhouse, and ended up choosing a beautiful ten-by-thirty-foot model that cost about $3000.

The carefully packaged greenhouse parts arrived by truck sometime during our first Maine summer. We were so preoccupied with the gardens that we simply stored the boxes until the harvest was nearly completed. Then we began construction along the southeast side of the farmhouse. We hired a backhoe to dig a trench for the concrete footing and the foundation, which we built ourselves from cement blocks. It took us about two months to finish the masonry, erect the aluminum framing, glaze the lights, and lay the brick floor, using bricks we had saved from the dismantled chimneys. The greenhouse was very beautiful. It was also very inefficient. We had chosen it uncritically from the standpoint of its function, having been won over completely by its visual design.

That first winter we had no plans to use the space, and so we closed it off from the main part of the house, but early the next spring we opened the double glass doors that led out from the kitchen, in the hopes of starting our seedlings in a place with appropriate light, ventilation, and humidity. When the days were sunny, the greenhouse was lovely, but during gray spells and after sunset, it lost large amounts of heat to the outside. We had not anticipated the heat loss through a single layer of ordinary glass, so our first job was to try to correct the structure's design. We cut long thin strips of wood and attached them to the insides of the aluminum supports, and then we stapled on clear plastic, forming a second skin for the whole greenhouse. This reduced the heat loss substantially, but it also ruined the beauty of the design.

Another thing that we learned the hard way was the fact that we can always buy, cut, and replace any of the flat pieces of glass that might break in the greenhouse, but when the graceful pieces of curved glass break, we are obliged to return to the manufacturer for new ones. Positioned as it is beneath a valley that runs from the front cape to the attached ell of the farmhouse, the greenhouse has several times been broken by ice falling off the roof.

Using what we learned from that first prefabricated greenhouse and from our first simple pole-and-plastic shelters, we have gone on to design a number of structures, some permanent and some temporary, in which to grow seedlings. The designs always evolve from some critical flaws in our previous attempts, but I think that we have settled on a few ideas that are sound.

Whether the structure is aluminum or wooden, any greenhouse should be glazed with thermal glass or with two skins, so the heat loss is reduced. Glass may be the most pleasing option, but there are also different fiberglass materials and greenhouse plastics that will function well. Freestanding greenhouses do not have to be transparent on all sides, and in harsh climates, where energy is most costly, it is advisable to position the greenhouse facing south, with the north wall closed and insulated.

For our wooden structures, we have tried to locate cedar, which can be milled into lumber with dimensional strength for the framework and also into one-inch boards from which we make plant tables (which we cover with wooden strips or hardware cloth). Cedar can withstand the constant humidity of a greenhouse without having to be treated with wood preservatives.

All of our greenhouses are heated with wood-burning stoves or furnaces. This has seemed the most economical choice, but it does mean that during exceptionally cold nights in March and sometimes in April, we have to rouse ourselves out of a warm bed to trudge out to stoke the fires. We have never had any back-up heating systems that can take over if the weather gets very cold, and we are considering putting in some small oil heaters to relieve us from those midnight rounds. Whether you heat with wood or another system, it is necessary to assess how big the unit should be, and fans are always a necessity for good air circulation.

Large containers of water will do a lot of work in storing daytime heat. I recall building our first solar greenhouse and moving plants in on the same day that we finished setting up the stove. The greenhouse measured sixteen by thirty-two feet, and with the cold, windy March night, we were just able to keep the plants from freezing until the next day, when we moved in a half-dozen fifty-five-gallon drums filled with water. The water heated up during the day and slowly released its warmth at night. In addition, we have tried suspending barrels of water on iron cradles over the woodstoves, so that the water was heated at night by the fire and we had warm water each morning to mix with the cold well water that we used to water our plants.

If you are a backyard gardener, it is likely that you will first be seduced into thinking about a greenhouse by any one of a number of ads that appear constantly in the glossy magazines. By all means consider these, but at the same time check the yellow pages of any large city directory to find a greenhouse supplier, and go look at the things that it offers its customers, who are almost exclusively commercial growers. In addition, do some research in your local library, because there are endless numbers of articles on greenhouse designs, including everything from those that you can buy prefabricated to those that you can build completely on your own. We did not go about building our greenhouses this methodically, and we made some costly mistakes.

Our greenhouse space is complemented by a number of cold

frames. Some are freestanding, and we use them for perennials and annuals once the nighttime temperatures are acceptable. Then there are those we call our heat-assisted cold frames, built along the southern walls of the greenhouses. These cold frames are structured like any others, except that their back wall is the bottom front wall of the greenhouse. We set two to three windows into this wall and fasten a small fan on a thermostatic control facing into the cold-frame area. During the cold weather, we leave the covers on the frames, and during the coldest nights the thermostat activates the fan to draw heat out of the greenhouse and circulate it throughout the cold frame. (This notion is easily adaptable to most homes, since the cold frame can be placed on the south side of the house against a basement window, with a similar thermostat and fan.) This kind of cold frame is a halfway house, if you will, between the full protection of the greenhouse and the final hardening-off temperatures of the regular cold frames. These environments allow us to move plants out of the most-expensive-to-maintain greenhouses much sooner, and the gradual move from germination to hardening off and field transplanting gives us uncommonly hardy and healthy stock.

For the greenhouse we use for sowing our original seed flats, from which we transplant all our seedlings, we have decided that heat mats are essential on all the germinating benches. The initial costs of these mats are more than offset by the money we do not have to spend to keep the greenhouse temperature so high. Germinating seeds need not so much a high ambient air temperature as a consistently warm soil temperature. With heat mats under the flats, we can adjust and maintain a steady soil temperature so that germination is faster and more even, and the vigorous initial growth produces plants that are hardy and less susceptible to disease and insect damage. Home growers will probably have the best luck with starting their own plants over heat mats and in cold frames, if they can curb their impulse to seed too early in the spring; the most common error I hear about from home growers is that they simply cannot wait to plant something, so they inevitably end up with leggy, malnourished seedlings that struggle to survive in the inadequate light and humidity of a kitchen windowsill.

All of our experiments in attempting to produce healthy plants and large garden yields are based on some information that we digested years ago from our reading. A seed, once germinated, struggles to grow steadily into plant, flower, and fruit in an attempt to produce another seed and thus insure its survival. Every effort that can be made to assist that process and to guarantee smooth and continuous growth will result in the healthiest and most vigorous individuals. Whatever is done by nature or by intent to intervene in that process will have some effect on the eventual success of the plant.

To understand this helps to explain why all of us have purchased healthy-looking seedlings from a garden center and then, when these seedlings haven't produced well, said that we simply don't have green thumbs. The reasons people fail with plants may be their own mistakes. It may also be that these plants have already been stressed and manipulated by previous growers. There are many ways of delaying and stimulating plant growth through the use of light, temperature, water, and growth hormones. The plants may look healthy and well formed when they go on sale, but their ability to flower and fruit can be significantly affected by their early growing conditions. If the variety is not truly adaptable to the region you live in, the external appearance of the seedling will tell you nothing about its ability to succeed. These are just a few of the reasons we began and continue to try to understand the biological requirements of each seed and plant. It is also why we choose to grow our own seedlings, because our income is tied to getting maximum performance from our crops. If you don't grow your own garden stock, you need to know something about the methods used to produce these plants.

At the same time that we were developing gardening methods and working with planting techniques, we had to begin to educate ourselves in the purchase and use of farm machinery. The first thing we bought was a small Farmall tractor, manufactured sometime in the early forties. A farmer in one of the neighboring towns was selling it, complete with plows, harrow, cultivators, and mowing machine, for $1200. When the machine was delivered, we spread the attachments out on the side lawn and struggled to figure out what the different bent and curved pieces of metal were for. It's amusing to think back on those times, and it helps to explain why I now take pride in recognizing machines sitting around other farmyards. I'm pleased with the literacy I have developed with plants, machines, and the jargon of farming.

Initially, it was quite a thrill to own our own tractor. We could plough, harrow, and cultivate when we wanted the work done, and were not dependent on the availability of hired help. But beyond the practical advantages, there was the basic pleasure of learning to drive and operate large equipment. Now we were able to cut over small pieces of a new field and pull stumps out with chains attached to the work bar of the tractor. We could move some stones out of garden space and repair damaged stone walls with them. In some instances we used the tractor to skid wood from land that was not too hilly. We fabricated homemade trailers to haul behind it and used them to carry wood, tools, large quantities of plants, and produce.

The next significant piece of equipment that we purchased was a garden tiller, for working smaller areas of land and for cultivating parts of the field. We also bought a single-row potato digger, which we used for two seasons before we decided that we would not continue to raise large potato crops; so we sold the digger.

It was probably inevitable that we would next need our own welder, not just to repair the machinery that we had but also to design and build farm implements. Each of the new machines allowed us to do an enormous amount of work, and it is easy to see how people can be beguiled into thinking that newer, bigger, more sophisticated tools are essential. Mark and I have stood gaping at the equipment on display at the annual agricultural trade shows, imagining what we could accomplish if we had this or that. But in most cases the machinery has been too big for the parcels of land that we cultivate, and is really not suited to the goals of our farm.

We have also come to realize that most large machinery is used to perform specific tasks either on an irregular basis or once a year, at most. We have had to have stumps and stones bulldozed on occasion. We have had to move piles of wood with the use of a cherry picker — the crane mounted on the top of a pulp truck. We have had to reroute a part of a road into our farm, and we have had to hire a backhoe to dig trenches for water pipes and septic systems for new farm buildings.

Each spring we need to spread many tons of manure and lime onto the gardens and pastures. And whenever we clear out and turn over a new piece for cultivation, we must either plough and harrow repeatedly with our small Farmall or hire a large tractor and tiller to chew up the sod and roots so that we can seed an initial cover crop. Often it has been attractive to think that by owning a fairly large assortment of machinery, we would be able to accomplish much more work, in addition to having the flexibility to do the work whenever we choose. But the other side of that capability is the need to purchase, house, maintain, and operate the machinery ourselves.

After more than a decade of owning, renting, and borrowing sizable machinery, we have revised some of our original thinking about machines. We still have the tractor, the tiller, the welder, and a four-wheel-drive pickup — machines that we use repeatedly each season. It is unlikely that we will add to that equipment with anything more than a small bucket loader for the tractor. Our lime is spread by the company from which we purchase it. Our bulldozing and large tractor work is done by farmers or contractors in the area. Whenever possible, we exchange the use of machinery for our own work; for instance, we grow a variety of field seedlings for a farmer who lets us use his large tractor and manure spreader once each season.

Over the years, my thrill with using large machines has drastically decreased. Given the choice, I would work with my hands and stand or walk for days on end before spending a day in the seat of a machine. I have grown to dislike the noise of engines, which drowns out the sounds of the wind, insects, and birds. I resent the smell of exhaust, which overshadows the marvelous fragrances of the earth and plants. One year we borrowed a very up-to-date field transplanting machine, thinking that if it worked out well, we might consider buying our own. I spent days bumping along in a metal chair, feeding seedlings into rotating rubber grippers that in turn moved the plants down and into the ground. It was miserable. I felt very uncomfortable being distanced from the small plants, and wanted to tuck each one into the earth myself. When we had finished planting with the machine, I still felt the need to go over to each seedling and adjust the angle of the planting and tamp the soil firmly around the stem.

So if I can calculate that I will be able to do the same amount of work manually as with a machine, I will choose the former, both because it is more aesthetically pleasing for me and because the physical work of farming keeps my body in shape. Mark has also grown less eager to spend time on the machinery. We still have to do routine maintenance, but there is usually a willing newcomer who is happy to climb into the seat of the Farmall for a day of plowing or harrowing, and we are only too ready to accept.

The attitudes that one develops about working with machinery are probably more important than I would have imagined, and in our case they have profoundly affected the kind of farm we are developing. The fact that we continue to farm more intensively on a smaller and smaller scale is a response to the ways in which we prefer to work. Five years ago, we thought that all of the cleared eight acres would be just large enough to sustain our needs. Now we are using some of the land for pasture and for rotating our crops. We have adequate space for green manuring and soil building. The business is growing larger, but that is because we are scaling down and expanding the products from our crops.

The largest sum of money that we have ever spent on a single piece of equipment went for something that has to be kept as far away from dirt as possible. It also does more work for us than any other tool on the farm. We use the computer daily now for any number of farm-related tasks: for writing books, catalogues, and articles; for record keeping; and for analyzing data on ordering, planting, harvesting, selling, payroll, and taxes. The computer surprised me; I was reluctant even to consider buying it, and more reluctant still to sit down and confront it. I was less intimidated by the prospect of learning to assemble the implements of the tractor than I was to tackle keyboard commands. But like all new tools, if appropriate to the tasks, the computer soon became familiar and indispensable.

The need to educate ourselves about plants, farming methods, and equipment was a response to taking the problem of making a living off the land more and more seriously. I have no doubt that we will continue to learn and to revise our thinking in each of these areas. They are simply the prerequisites for surviving. But the most important thing that we had to confront and begin to understand was the area of marketing. In fact, early on in our farming, we never even used the word *marketing*. We simply sold our produce.

By the summer of 1978 we were taking our vegetables and seedlings to markets in Auburn, Lewiston, Rumford, and Portland. Since the Lewiston and Portland markets both took place on Saturday, Mark took one truck and I took another, borrowed from my parents, and we each set off early in the morning. We usually sold the better part of our vegetables, but the effort that it took to pick, sort, pack, set up, repack, and drive was tremendous. On the days when we brought back hundreds and hundreds of dollars, we were able to justify the effort, but on days when the weather was too rainy, too cold, or too hot, we had to expend the same amount of work for customers who didn't show up to buy.

From the money we made and saved that first summer and fall, we had to apportion funds to carry us over until the next season. The first winter was a real test of our commitment. We were determined to use little or no oil for heating, but we did not find time to cut or haul any wood until December, after we finished building the glass greenhouse. That meant that we spent many days hauling in green wood through increasingly deep snow, first with the tractor, then with the truck, and finally with toboggans. The farmhouse was uninsulated, except for the kitchen, which we rebuilt, and when the wind blew, we could feel it inside. During the coldest spells, frost appeared on some of the north-facing inside walls. Still, we were determined not to use any oil, and anyway we had very little money to use for fuel. We set up four small old wood-burning stoves, collected from auctions and barn sales, and we spent hours every day stoking stoves, carrying wood to both floors of the farmhouse, and carrying and cleaning ashes and wood chips. At no expense to our cash reserve but at great expense to our time and energy, we kept warm enough, but after one winter we resolved never again to heat our house with a series of small stoves.

The next season we purchased a wood-burning furnace, and Mark installed it himself, using the existing ductwork from the central oil burner. At the base of the decision to save up enough money to purchase and use a wood-burning furnace, which cost $2000, was the whole question of what goods and materials we needed to free us up for other things, and, conversely, how much money we needed to earn to purchase those goods. It's a delicate balancing act, managing work in order to purchase, and doing without for the sake of having time.

We had such a limited income that first winter that we had to budget every expense, right down to how many gallons of milk we bought in a given week. We decided to make all of the gifts we gave during the holiday season, so we went to a nearby tannery and bought leather skins, from which we designed belts, vests, and a briefcase. We gave presents from our pantry of jams and jellies, pickles and relishes. I really did not feel that we were sacrificing, despite our lack of money, but I did begin to take more seriously the fact that we *had* to make a minimum amount of money from the crops, and that each year there would be endless uncontrollable variables that could affect our income. In short, no one was taking care of us anymore. For a reasonable day's work, there would be no guaranteed paycheck, no medical care, no expense accounts, and, not least of all, no status.

We watched our vegetable yields increase, but even when we worked out that we could produce more than $5000 worth of mixed crops per acre, there was a limit to the acreage two of us could manage and to the efforts that we could sustain. At best, we could count on a respectable income from late June until late October, but with the increasing costs of seed, gasoline, and machinery maintenance, along with general living expenses, we needed to find other ways to bring in money from work on the farm. The alternative was to settle on the realization that we would always have to have outside work to support ourselves.

I am not certain which of these influences played the strongest part in our drive to make the farm the major focus of our work, but both the wish to free ourselves from having to work for others and the wish to define some series of endeavors that would give us interesting and satisfying work, and at least a degree of solvency, played a part. Only a short time out of the city, we began to articulate the challenge as we saw it and to invest ourselves even more seriously in defining a life that was focused entirely on horticulture.

This much was becoming clear: farming for a living cannot be done casually in this climate. The season is too short, the soil is too tired, and the markets are too far away. We were going to have to analyze and apply whatever information or imaginative thinking we could find to give us a chance to continue.

6 · FULL-TIME FARMERS

LAST EVENING Roger, Pam, Ann, Mark, and I gathered in the summer room of the farmhouse for dinner. There was one other guest, but Bob had never worked at Hedgehog Hill, so he was an onlooker, or perhaps our audience, for the several hours of reminiscing. The memories were sometimes tender, sometimes painful, and, as the evening wore on, increasingly hilarious. Each of us was picking through our experiences, choosing to relive some and, I'm certain, remembering but choosing not to talk about others. At one point in the evening, I turned to Ann and asked her if she had ever imagined that we would sit around like this, talking and laughing about our years of working together. She replied that yes, she had known we would, but she had been uncertain how long it would take to get to that point. For Roger, Mark, and me, it had been a long time, because Roger was our first full-time employee at Hedgehog Hill. It has now been four

years since Roger left the farm to become a manager for one of
the Maine Arby's restaurant franchises, and it has been eight
years since we first met him.

In the spring of 1979, Mark and I were looking for someone to
cut and clear the wood from a badly overgrown field that lay
southeast of the farmhouse. We asked around our neighborhood
to see if any of the woodcutters might be interested in clearing
the land, in exchange for either wood or pay. Roger Crockett, the
son-in-law of one of our neighbors, came by to inquire about the
work. Our first meeting was somewhat uncomfortable. We had
not really anticipated hiring another adult to work full-time on
the farm. We had not thought through our expectations about
work or about money. The discussion was a kind of exchange of
ideas between us and Roger, and each was cautiously trying to
get a sense of the other.

Roger was very guarded with us at first, and we later learned
that he saw the differences in our backgrounds as real barriers
to our understanding and appreciation of each other. He was born
and raised in this area and had traveled out of Maine infrequently.
He and his family were members of the local evangelical church,
and his political and social attitudes were at the time strictly
formed by his wish to be associated with the church's conservative doctrine. He had recently left a job selling ax handles manufactured by a local company, and he was looking for part-time
and odd jobs to support himself, his wife, and their three children.

Roger's impressions of us were formed primarily from the local
gossip, which we learned from him years later. It seems that Mark
and I were commonly referred to as the foreigners, or the hippies
from the city who had come to farm. We were said to be unorthodox, politically radical, and most of all different. According
to rumor, we also had quite a bit of money, because everyone
knew you couldn't farm for a living in Maine, especially with an
organic vegetable farm.

Despite our apparent differences, the three of us muddled through
a kind of mutual interview, and Roger agreed to take on the work

of clearing for an hourly wage. The area that he had to cut and clear covered about six sloping acres. That section of the farm had once been used for corn and bean production, and the land still bore the scars of continuous plowing and soil erosion. Whoever had discontinued the vegetable farming had then set out an orchard of standard apple trees, but this too had been ignored long enough for invading poplars to grow thirty to forty feet tall and for some of the white birches to measure a foot in diameter. There was also an unsightly growth of scrub pine, alders, brambles, and gray birch. All in all, it was the kind of cutting that left you with a sizable portion of brush and lesser amounts of usable wood.

Roger began work in April. We watched him come and go each day, carrying his chain saw, gas cans, and lunch box across the back lawn and up into the field. We heard him nearly all day; the saw quieted down only when he was stacking logs or piling brush. As the weeks passed, we tried to get him to join us for lunch, but he was reluctant to come down off the land. Little by little, though, the field began to take form, and so did our acquaintance. In three months Roger completely cleared the whole parcel, and very neatly stacked the four-foot lengths of usable wood and piled the brush in long narrow rows for burning. It was an impressive piece of clearing, carefully done by someone who obviously took great pride in his work.

I don't remember when Roger first agreed to have lunch with us, but gradually during those three months we began to break from work and sit out on the lawn or in the kitchen to eat and talk together. Initially we spoke mainly of the work he was doing, of the weather, of the projects that Mark and I were working on. Gradually, as we felt more comfortable with each other, we talked about our backgrounds, our past jobs and families, our plans, and the coincidence of our having left the city and his having left a steady job for what each of us hoped would be a more interesting way of making a living. Our opportunities to watch each other work, to talk about and share some common ideas and goals, began to overshadow the differences in our backgrounds and in our political and religious beliefs. Our getting acquainted was strongly based on our shared belief in hard work, on our pride in the quality of that work, and on our similar hopes for carving out new lives not totally defined by nine-to-five institutions.

By the time Roger finished the cutting, Mark and I had decided to ask him whether he would be interested in staying on for as many months as possible to work with us in the fields. At that point, neither Mark nor I was certain how much labor we could afford, or how interested we were in a full-time commitment. Roger too was not interested in taking on a full-time job, but he liked the idea of working for a few months and then having the winter to find jobs with some of the woodsmen in the area.

Prior to Roger's arrival, Mark and I had solved our labor needs with an extraordinary amount of help from my parents. Although my parents have always wondered why we wanted to give up the life we had in the city to work manually on a farm, they have always supported our efforts with many hours of help. Before we moved permanently to Maine, my mother drove to the farm every Friday to supervise the picking of some of the vegetables for the weekend farmers' markets (we hired a few young people to work in the fields when the crops needed harvesting). My parents also farm-sat at critical times during the season. When we left seedlings unattended during our work week in the city, they checked on the watering and put blankets and cloches over tender seedlings or field transplants if frosts threatened. Perhaps because of these many hours of volunteer help, we still saw our operation as a family farm — a small and private undertaking.

After our first season of trying to raise crops for farmers' markets on a full-time basis, Mark and I considered hiring another person, but the transition from having a private family farm to having a real employee was a big step. Hiring Roger for a specific task, which gave us the chance to get used to having another person working on our land, was our way of easing into the change. In fact, when Roger came to cut the wood, we had no notion of asking him to stay on. We watched him work, and he watched us work. The decision to ask him to join us grew naturally out of a trial period.

I never would have believed that another worker could make such a difference to the productivity of a place. Simple mathematics says that one added to two should increase the output by fifty percent. But the three of us as a team could easily do twice as much planting, tilling, hoeing, harvesting, building, cutting, and selling. It was not just the simple fact that there was another body to work; it was the difference that another person, particularly a person from outside the family, made in a workplace that had been up to that time a personal one. After Roger joined us, we were no longer a family farm. When decisions had to be made about planting, work schedules, machinery use, or whatever, they were made by and affected not a couple but a small group of workers. Mark and I could no longer conduct our days in accordance with our personal whims and habits; we had to organize our work to accommodate the presence of another person. In every sense, we were no longer just a couple who were farming, and we had to begin to examine the ways in which our personal dynamics affected the workplace of another person.

The hiring of a third person was one of the most significant changes we made in our country work. Furthermore, it gave us a different economic responsibility, one we only began to appreciate after the first year or so, as our commitment to Roger grew and our dependence on one another increased. When times were tight and income diminished, we needed to hang on to a certain amount of money to pay Roger. When the income was increased by midseason vegetable sales, we needed to squirrel away enough money to have on hand for ourselves and for Roger's wages. Roger also came to rely on the farm income for his family. It was no longer a matter of Mark and me and Jacob living frugally, with the insurance of other professions to back us up if the farm didn't work out. We had undertaken the responsibility of caring for another family, and at least in part we began to think about the

ways in which we could insure a regular income throughout the
year.

This realization that our farm had changed from a personal
enterprise to a small business was not in the least burdensome,
because the responsibilities were constantly offset by the amaz-
ing increase in our collective productivity. That first summer
the three of us, still with help from my parents, were able to
grow, harvest, and market enough produce to more than double
our farm income.

We also began to expand our methods of selling produce and
products from the farm. In fact, the opportunity to market our
vegetables and flowers to a wholesale buyer came quite effort-
lessly. The local extension agent, with whom we were in constant
contact at the farmers' markets, called to tell us that the owners
of Maine's three Arby's restaurants were looking for locally grown
produce. Were we interested in talking with Ken Raffel, one of
the owners? With the attitude of "nothing ventured," Mark set
up a meeting at the Auburn franchise — the one that Roger now
manages.

Mark was enthusiastic when he returned from the meeting.
He had learned that Ken and his brother, Jim, were sons of the
founder of Arby's, and when they decided to settle in Maine with
their families, they bought three franchises in the state. Their
social and political commitments encouraged them to support
local farming and food manufacturing (they have in fact led the
way in the state for such support), and they wanted a local supplier for some of their vegetables.

Other farmers at the markets were also told about the wholesale opportunity, but everyone else shunned the idea of doing
business with local restaurants. They were cynical about our
interest and enthusiasm, but we felt optimistic about the possibilities of a known market for a fairly predictable amount of
vegetables. Unlike some of the other farmers in our area, we had
no history of wholesale agreements gone sour. We had never
grown large amounts of vegetables only to have the prospective

buyer change his mind and refuse to take the produce. We were responding to the offer with a naive trust that the agreement could be made to work. Moreover, we could quite accurately project our gardening needs, because the restaurants were able to provide us, a year in advance, with projected usage figures for all the things that they would like to purchase from our farm. So, based on our belief in the sincerity of the offer, we planned our next garden both to supply the restaurant orders and to continue our sales at three farmers' markets.

Roger, Mark, and I worked together for the remainder of that first summer and fall, until wood began to be hauled in for the winter and Roger left for three months to free-lance as a woodsman. In March he returned, and the three of us began building our first permanent greenhouse, one that would include our ideas on passive solar heating, with a back-up wood heating system. We had to hire a bulldozer to move the two feet of snow that remained on the ground before we could lay out a foundation, which that year consisted of a simple wooden plate leveled on top of rocks and cement blocks. We had cedar milled for the framing, and we glazed the front, south-facing wall with rigid greenhouse fiberglass. We finished construction just in time to begin transplanting the seedlings we were growing both for ourselves and for selling at the farmers' markets. The income from seedling sales that year just about covered the cost of building the greenhouse.

At first the new greenhouse space seemed more than adequate, but our ambitions seem to keep full pace with our expansion, and the next year we were quickly erecting another greenhouse. That season we had neither the time nor the money to build a proper structure, so we hurriedly erected a pole greenhouse with newly cut young trees. The poles were no sooner cleaned than they were set in place, and in fact some of them sprouted branches that summer. We studded the roof with two-by-eights and closed in the building with six-mil plastic.

Since we were pressed for growing space, plastic and fiberglass structures were put up rather quickly on the back lawn of our farmhouse. The mixture of reasonably designed and slapdash greenhouses was certainly never beautiful, but the buildings allowed us to expand our spring seedling business and to experiment with different varieties of vegetables, flowers, and herbs. More than anything, the new space fed our growing enthusiasm for working with plants.

Spring became a favorite time at the farm for all three of us. Sowing the seed flats, watching for the first cotyledons, waiting for the emergence of true leaves, and the ensuing frenzy of trying to transplant thousands of young plants kept us so busy that our farming season quite naturally expanded back into February. With the need for working in the field all summer, harvesting into the fall, and cutting wood until sometime in November, there was soon a permanent job for Roger at the farm.

After the first season of delivering vegetables to three restaurants and three farmers' markets, we examined the efforts it had taken to maintain all these accounts. It was more work than we felt we could sustain, so we pulled out of one farmers' market. At the same time, we expanded our wholesale business by contracting for sales with a few other restaurants located along the delivery route to Arby's.

In addition, we started to manufacture our first farm product when we began processing our cabbage into coleslaw for Arby's — a suggestion that came from the restaurants' owners. Before investing in a commercial cabbage shredder, we actually sliced some twelve hundred pounds of cabbage on an old single-blade wooden hand shredder, and grated carrots with a small kitchen tool. We experimented with several different slaw recipes and packaging techniques before coming up with a consistently good product that the restaurants said they would be willing to purchase on a regular basis. The slaw, made from green and purple cabbage and carrots, sold for fifty cents a pound, whereas the cabbage alone brought in only about fifteen cents a pound at the farmers' markets. But as important as the increase in price was the fact that the demand for coleslaw lasted all season, and we figured we could grow hundreds of winter-storage cabbages and process slaw during the fall and early winter, when income from vegetables had ended.

We went ahead and purchased a commercial shredder and began to make thousands of pounds of coleslaw. The most significant thing about this undertaking was the notion that we could look at all of our produce from the standpoint of whether it could be turned into products. If we could manufacture products, we could perhaps increase the farm income and keep labor on the farm for a longer work year. Furthermore, if we could grow crops that could be manufactured during off-season months, then we had the chance to develop the farm into a year-round business. These are probably obvious concepts to any business-minded person, but for us the discovery was exciting and encouraging.

The profile of our farm was becoming more complex. The three of us now had a small seedling business, a small vegetable farm, and a coleslaw manufacturing endeavor. All of this was run from the glass greenhouse that opened off our kitchen, the few structures on our back lawn, and very often the kitchen itself, where we washed, chopped, and bagged thousands of pounds of slaw from August until early January. There were some obvious drawbacks to having all of these operations in the middle of our home. For starters, you can't shred that much cabbage without its ending up all over the counters, walls, and floors of your house. Despite our best efforts to clean up after the work was done, the remnants of rapidly deteriorating cabbage leaves gave off a fragrance that overtook the farmhouse. Our physical facilities were sorely inadequate, and Mark and I soon grew impatient with the situation. It was becoming apparent that we needed another building.

In the spring of 1980 we began the first farm project to be done by outside contractors, who laid the footing and foundation for our barn in the northeast corner of our major production field.

We drew up plans for a two-story, gambrel-roofed structure, where we dreamed we would keep crops, process food, store tools and machinery, and repair automotive and farm machinery. We cut lumber from our own land and had it milled into heavy structural timbers — six-by-tens for floor supports, two-by-sixes for studding, and different one-inch boards for finishing. When the cutting and milling was done, we ran out of money to go beyond capping the foundation with a first floor. It was the last fall work for that year, completed after the wood was in and just before the snows began. We finished in time to cover the floor with a large sheet of plastic, which we anchored down with old tires. That left us just enough money to get us through the winter and purchase seeds for the next season.

Late in the winter of 1980, we put together a rather plainly designed, home-typed couple of pages listing the seedlings we planned to offer at the farm that spring. We reproduced the pages on the mimeograph machine at the local high school and distributed copies to every neighbor and friend and to all the customers at the farmers' market for whom we had names and addresses. We called the mailing our seedling preorder package, and it invited customers to place plant orders early in the spring at a reduced price. We figured that we could plan our seedling business more accurately if we could encourage customers to order early. Their orders would give us some notion of what our total spring plant sales might be. It would also commit customers to purchasing their seedlings from our farm, instead of buying them on impulse from their local gardening centers. Furthermore, by asking for a small deposit with each order, we could generate a bit of working capital early in the season. The first year's response was modest: about two dozen people told us what plants they would like to have ready in May.

The next season we produced a more elaborate seedling mailer, and orders doubled. That was the year we planned an open house, to show off our new greenhouse and cold frames and to try to stimulate plant sales on the farm rather than at the farmers' markets. Our invitation for the open house went out in the form of a flier, and we also put several small ads in the local newspapers. We scheduled the event for a Saturday and Sunday in the middle of May. We had no idea what the turnout would be.

I clearly remember watching the road early that Saturday morning, waiting and wondering whether anyone would show up. Cars began to drive down the road. The first ones belonged mainly to friends and neighbors who had come to support us. Then there were cars containing members of the community who were curious as to who we were and what we were doing with the old Turner farm. More cars arrived, with people we had met at various farmers' markets. They wanted to see where we lived and where we grew the food they had been purchasing for the past several years. By Sunday evening the event had attracted two or three hundred people, and we had served as many cups of coffee and tea and homemade cookies. As an opening gambit, it had been very successful, not to mention a good deal of fun. We met dozens of community families, many of them on Sunday, after word of mouth had prompted their curiosity. I am fairly certain that many of our Sunday visitors showed up to sample the free refreshments rather than to purchase plants, but whatever caused the turnout, we knew that the idea was valid and well worth continuing another year. Interestingly enough, there are very few spring events or fairs in Maine. The fall is replete with agricultural events, but there seems to be very little ritual for the spring, a time when even seasoned farmers are optimistic and backyard gardeners are committed to planting, weeding, and watering like never before.

Pam came that year as well. She owned a farm about twenty miles from ours, and raised over a hundred head of Hereford and Angus, three hundred laying hens, and lesser amounts of pigs and ducks. In addition, she studied music and gave occasional piano concerts, and sometimes designed clothing for herself and a few friends. We had met originally at a meeting of local farmers, and Mark and I asked her if she would like to sell some of her eggs during our open house.

The friendship between Pam and Mark and me did not begin cautiously or slowly. She was for me, at last, another woman living in the country, a woman with enormous energy who shared my interests. The women I had come to know and admire in the city were as busy with their lives as I was with mine, and over the years we were in touch less and less. Since coming to the country, I had not met many other women as interested as I was in agriculture and the arts. Several women were involved in homesteading, but that usually meant that their affinity was for the traditional homemaking skills, and thus I often had little in common with them.

Pam was also looking for people who could understand her particular combination of interests and who could appreciate the strong bond one forms with a place in the country. She and her husband had retreated to the country to raise cattle. When they separated, Pam stayed at the farm with their son, Aaron, and tried to run the whole operation, raise a small child, and keep up her involvement in music and painting. She was torn between holding onto a physically and economically difficult beef farm and trying to establish herself as a clothing designer. It was a dilemma that took her years to unravel, and during that time our friendship grew and matured.

When Mark and I repeated our open house the following spring, we called it an open house/spring fair. We liked the idea of including other exhibitors and invited a few potters, basketmakers, collectors of antique tools, and wool producers to join in. The crowds increased rapidly, as did our preorder seedling business. All of this was assisted by the attention brought to our farm from a couple of newspaper articles that had appeared the previous year. Pam came again with her eggs, having sold off her cattle as a first step toward ending the agricultural business and making the transition to designing. She also brought along a few of her designed clothes. Nikki came with handmade quilted hangings.

David brought his silver jewelry. Johnny's Selected Seeds had a good display of seeds, garden tools, and books. There were maple-syrup producers and craftspeople with toys and wooden items. On Saturday it was cold and rainy, but customers came anyway, so we frantically cleaned out the rooms on the first floor of our farmhouse and moved the craftspeople inside. Sunday turned out sunny and warm, and everyone went back outdoors. Perhaps there are few spring fairs because there is a very good possibility of rain and an absolute certainty of blackflies. But the people who continue to attend our fairs over the years joke goodheartedly about the weather and the flies, and the meek simply stay away.

For three summers Pam worked with us at the farm on a part-time basis. During that time the focus of work gradually began to change, and our interest in flowers and herbs evolved. We included fresh and a few everlasting flowers in our field production so that we could offer bouquets to customers at farmers' markets and to restaurants. At first we grew the most common annuals and perennials, but we expanded the planting each year, so that we soon were growing more than two dozen varieties of everlastings alone. The everlasting bouquets were very popular, especially during the fall market sales.

I'll never forget making my first herbal wreath. Mark and I were asked by a local food cooperative to talk about growing and drying herbs and flowers, a subject that we knew a little about. I was also asked to demonstrate herbal wreath making, a subject I knew nothing about. I had once examined a wreath made of very delicate artemisias and small everlastings, and I decided that I could probably reproduce the process. I took an old coathanger, fashioned it into a circle, and crimped it with a pair of pliers. Then I cut picture-hanging wire into uniform lengths, clustered stems of herbs and everlastings, and wired the bunches onto the wire circle. But my folly was in trying to tie a wreath for the first time while talking to a small group assembled at the food coop. The audience was polite, and I remember everyone saying that the wreath was quite beautiful. In fact, I too thought that it came out well, and after the demonstration I gave the wreath to my parents. They hung it in their home. A few years later I looked at it much more critically, and now I wonder how I had the nerve to demonstrate its design in public.

I went on to make many hundred more wreaths, and so did my mother, to whom I showed my technique, and so did Pam. Over time, the wreaths improved considerably, and with our expanding varieties of herbs and everlastings, we were able to design bouquets and wreaths that were fairly unusual. Using a few photographs of our work, Mark and I submitted our everlastings to a jury for acceptance into the Common Ground Country Fair, which is probably the largest rural and crafts fair for the granola crowd in the state. Some thirty to forty thousand people now attend this fall fair each year, and the exhibitors include some of the best craftspeople in the state.

When we applied in 1981, there were very few people working with everlastings, and we were delighted to be accepted. For several weeks, my mother, Pam, and I tied and decorated herbal wreaths, Roger, Mark, Pam, and I assembled bouquets, carefully wrapped them in white tissue paper, and tied them with ribbons. Then we set up a booth at our first big crafts fair. Since we had the only booth offering everlastings, we sold over two hundred bouquets, several dozen wreaths, and a few dried herbs for cooking, and took home over $2000 after three days of exhibiting.

That same fall Mark took some samples of our work to a few craft stores and boutiques in Maine and in the Boston area, and we got our first wholesale orders. The expansion of our farm into the growing and production of everlastings was a significant new venture, because now we had a crop that gave us the opportunity to manufacture and market all through the winter.

At some time in the early stages of our dried-flower business, I remember, Mark said that there must be manufactured wire frames for making wreaths and why didn't I call up some floral suppliers and inquire. I replied that it was just as easy to bend and crimp old coathangers, which was easy for me to say, because as our production increased, this was a job that Mark ended up having to do. But when I began to work with small arrangements of dried materials, I had to rummage around in our attic or in secondhand shops to find containers which I could fill with newspaper or sand to hold the flower stems. One day, out of sheer desperation, Mark hunted through the yellow pages of a Portland telephone directory and called a wholesaler of floral supplies to ask whether they carried wreath frames and baskets we could purchase. The industry came driving down our road — a fully stocked brown van and a sales representative named Tillie. It was quite a revelation to learn that a whole industry existed to sell endless sizes of wreath frames, floral tape, floral picks, foam bricks for flower arranging, ribbons, baskets, pottery, and whatever else you might need. It was also a huge relief to Mark to be freed from transforming all of our coathangers into wreath frames.

As our dried-flower production grew, we were extremely lucky to have Pam on the staff and my mother available for so many hours each week. Each of these women has an uncommon talent for working with flowers and colors, and there I was working as a designer again, now with flowers instead of magazines. Meanwhile, we had to maintain the seedling business, the field production, and the harvesting for restaurants and farmers' markets along with the burgeoning business with herbs and everlastings. The demands were often overwhelming, but we felt that there was some economic safety in having a number of small ventures that spread the income throughout the year. The farm was about as diversified as we could manage, and we were unwilling to let go of any aspect of the business. We needed more help.

Ann joined us for a summer only. She was and still is the librarian at a small community library about twenty miles from here. Like me, Ann made her way to Maine after years of urban experience, which included teaching in a private school in New York City. She requested a summer leave of absence from her library to work with us, as she was intrigued by the notion of farming. She could not have had a rougher initiation — the summer she joined us was perhaps one of the hardest we have ever had. Needless to say, we were overcommitted, and Mark and Roger and I were driving ourselves, trying to keep pace. That year we also had an infestation of cutworms unlike anything I've ever seen. Of every hundred plants we set out in the upper field, the cutworms chopped off twenty-five or thirty.

Then there was the woodchuck. We were planting several thousand heads of cabbage, broccoli, and cauliflower, primarily for the restaurant deliveries. The woodchuck was so bold that after a morning of transplanting, when we returned to the field after our lunch break, the animal had mowed down a good part of what we had set out. To make things more difficult, I was vehemently opposed to shooting any animal. Everyone else indulged my attitude, and we set out milk bottles painted black to frighten off the invader. Those worked for about two days; then he was right back eating again. Finally I had to face the choice of losing all our income from the crops or killing the woodchuck. Everyone had long since lost patience with my pacifism at the expense of our gardens. But all that summer I felt sad about having to kill wildlife, and perhaps this led to my first inclinations to give up vegetable production, if it meant having to guard our income with a rifle. There are always a few rabbits and deer in the gardens, and even a few crows pulling out young corn, but we had never been sufficiently bothered to trap or shoot anything until that summer.

Even with five of us, Roger, Ann, Pam, Mark, and I were really pressed to plant, maintain, harvest, manufacture, and deliver our goods to the markets, restaurants, and shops that were carrying our things. It was a taxing time for all of us, both physically and emotionally. Ann worked extremely hard, and like us before her she watched her body become strong and muscled and her gardening abilities increase. She also knew clearly, long before the end of the summer, that she didn't want to be a farmer. At the end of her four-month stay, she was more than happy to return to the library.

We anticipated Ann's leaving, but while she was at the farm she gave enormous energy and commitment to her work. She also made some interesting observations about how people learn to recognize patterns of vegetative growth and plant maturity. She was able to verbalize the development of skills that the rest of us simply took for granted, and so we were able to relive our own growth through her training. We were sorry to see her go, disappointed that the summer had been so hard for her. It made us all reflect on our own attachment to farming. But at the same time, we had known that she was simply trying it out, and we were prepared for her return to the library.

Pam's commitment was always undefined, because she came to work and help out when it coincided with our needs and her availability. We gained so much from each other. She used our farm as a place to withdraw gradually from farm work after she sold off her cattle, then her chickens, and then the other farm animals. When we worked together on design projects, we were constantly able to draw similarities between designing with flowers and with fabric. The problems of textures, colors, forms, and techniques are the same whatever materials are being manipulated. When we worked, we nearly always listened to classical music on radio or tapes, and we chatted endlessly about music and politics. As her clothing business began to take shape, she had less time to spend here, but our friendship continues and our conversations now include the problems of managing small businesses.

When Pam first stopped working here, I missed her terribly. I wanted someone to bounce ideas off. I wanted someone to challenge my own developing style with everlastings. I wanted someone to listen to a piece of music with and to comment on its form. And although I can and do share all of these thoughts with Mark, I realized that I missed another woman, and that the farm with Mark, Roger, and me had been a very male-oriented workplace.

Pam came and went gradually; Ann came and went after a defined period of time. But Roger came for an indefinite stay.

With Roger, Mark and I did the heaviest, hardest, most significant work of developing the farm into a real small business. We were all working harder than any three people should to make a diversified farm viable. In the process, we became totally involved in one another's lives and goals. Roger went through a troublesome separation and divorce, and for several months moved in with us while he tried to sort out where he wanted to live. When his personal life was most in turmoil, he hid himself in work, and the three of us labored relentlessly to build the wholesale businesses in food and everlastings. During that same period we completed the barn, and Mark finished his dissertation.

None of the three of us was ready for the inevitable: that Roger would one day wish to look for another job, for more opportunities for himself, and for the security of more money and the typical benefits of a traditional workplace. The separation was painful. Each of us felt so dependent on the others. Mark and I couldn't imagine doing all the work without Roger, because he was so much a part of the growth that he knew as well as we the schedule and demands of each season, of each day. And I'm certain that he felt loyal to the place and to us, having been a principal member. But in fact the farm was still a family farm, and there were only limited opportunities for someone else. It was really Mark and I who made the major decisions about money, direction, and goals. We were ultimately responsible for the day-to-day management decisions as other people joined the staff. Although Roger was given the job of field manager, he was still answerable to us, and the job became too small, too restrictive. It was time for him to look for a position with more potential. And even though we understood what was happening, and even though we had in fact done the same things ourselves during our twenties, Mark and I hated to see him leave.

We three manufactured some bad feelings around the time of leaving, much as small children manufacture an argument just before they know one of them has to go home. I guess it was our way of detaching. And yet the bad feelings were so overlaid with years of commitment to each other and to a project that none of us has wanted to let go of the friendship. We were very vulnerable to one another, and the understanding of that vulnerability has helped us to re-evaluate our relationships with many people who have since come to work with us.

I feel I have a few insights about workplaces, both those in which I have participated and the one I now direct with Mark. I also have some hopes for any group of people working together, and the hopes and the insights are sometimes at odds with each other. I thought that we could create a workplace where everyone felt equal, where everyone felt confident that his or her efforts were appreciated and respected. I wanted a place where people would have time to learn, to be stimulated by the sheer fact of learning. I wanted a workplace where people would take risks, take part in decision making, where things were very participatory.

At the same time, Mark and I are extremely strong-willed about most issues, very definite in our opinions and tastes, and totally caught up in the creation of a small business, from which we almost never take a break. No outside person should or can possibly be as involved as we are. No other person can know all of the things that we are thinking or planning, since so many of our discussions take place outside the boundaries of the traditional workday. And although the business finances have been fairly clearly reported to others on the staff, there is no way for them to know about or to worry about the weeks when cash simply doesn't appear or when the increasing costs of workman's compensation or insurance take their toll. No one can be as involved as we are. More important, we are the owners and therefore are inevitably seen as the people in charge, and we thus exercise a certain control over the lives of people with whom we are in daily contact.

Now we try to sort all of that out in establishing our relationships with the many people who come and go from the farm. This is a small and intimate place, and when our ranks are swelled by summer staff, we are still never more than a dozen people, including my parents. Working as closely together as we do, intimacy inevitably grows, as we talk about our lives, our families, our problems with money, health, friendships. But despite all of the time that we spend together outside of work — at each other's homes for dinner, swapping child care, at concerts, at movies — we are still aware of the hierarchy in our working relationships.

In addition, every employee brings to the workplace a certain set of expectations. When the business is small and family-owned, chances are that the owners are overly committed to its success. Everyone who comes to work here sees that we work hard nearly all of the time, and by inference gets the impression that he or she is expected to work that hard. In fact, when we interview people now, we tell them that we are hard-working to a fault, and that unless they are comfortable in a place of high expectations, they will be unhappy at the farm. People never understand the full import of that warning. Some see it as a challenge. Some ignore it, thinking that they will find their own pace here, when we are all doing as much as possible to insure each little part of the business.

One year we had to let someone go, after allowing a bad situation to deteriorate for much too long. A new person on the staff was really trying to coast on the work of everyone else. Inexperienced in the skills of managing a group of people, Mark and I tried to talk with this person, who listened well and talked a good line but in the end was not able to take himself or the job as seriously as the rest of us did. Other people on the staff that summer were angry at having to make up work for someone else, and equally angry with Mark and me for letting ourselves be taken advantage of. Everyone's sense of himself and everyone's respect for us as the managers was diminished by a single individual. When we finally asked him to leave, we felt a combination of guilt, anger, and sadness for our own failure to deal early on with the difficulty of an employee who doesn't work out.

In my own experience as an employee, I always complained that people forget to praise each other for good work but are never slow to criticize. Knowing that full well, I too sometimes forget that praise is needed by everyone, and particularly by the people who work for us. Everyone here is very sensitive to our interpretation of his or her work. More than that, everyone here is quick to interpret our personal moods as having something to do with our feeling about him or her. In such a small workplace, Mark and I have to be very careful of our personal interactions, because they affect everyone else. Conversely, we as employers are vulnerable to the moods and uneven work habits of others. How can we tell what is a bad day, a poor job, a waning of interest? How much are we responsible to the people at the farm, and how much of the normal fluctuations of mood and performance should we simply overlook and ascribe to the moons, the tides, and personal, nonfarm-related causes? This is always a real trick in a small community. We ask the people who come here to get involved and share in our rather improbable dream. Mark and I started out believing that a small, versatile farm could provide a living for a few people. That belief flies in the face of all odds, and yet we still hold on.

As the years have passed, we have continually modified our approach to hiring. It began casually, but we have since tried some very methodical approaches — ads in the newspapers, résumés, interviews, rating procedures, and careful evaluation. When we played out that procedure to its fullest, we had the most disastrous summer of all. As a friend once commented, perhaps it was because we got caught up in the process and focused less on the people than we should have.

There have been years when we swore strongly that we would not hire young people, because they lack commitment and reliability. We now have two high school students on the staff, and each of them comes back year after year. Their youthful insouciance and energy often provide the levity we need to get us through the hardest demands of the summer.

If I could draw one conclusion about the ways in which the best people have come to Hedgehog Hill, I guess it would have to be that word of mouth, happy coincidence, and chance encounters work well. The best people here have always been those we have asked to join us because we just trusted our instincts about them. Sometimes the people have had relevant work experience. Sometimes they have just been personally appealing, and we have carved out a job in order to have them on the staff.

When new people join us, we can usually tell early on whether the decision was a good one, and if we watch carefully, we can sometimes help shape a job to match that person's interests and skills. But whatever jobs each of us does on the farm, we are never far away from the nature of our business. And ultimately, if someone does not arrive with or develop a natural love of plants and the out-of-doors, then he or she will not stay long at Hedgehog Hill. So much of the work here is repetitive, physically difficult, tedious, and even mundane that the energy to do the work can only be sustained by a basic interest in the overall goals of the farm.

7 · MAKING CHANGES

ONE DAY Mark and I were sitting at the kitchen table with several years of farm records spread out before us. The discussion we were having was a familiar one: what would we do in the year ahead to improve our lives at the farm? We had now been living in Maine for four years, and our records told us that we had made some significant progress. But we had also worked inordinately hard for that progress, and in the process we had had to adjust our lives drastically to the realities of a rural income.

Mark was the first to come out with the question that had been nagging each of us privately, and once he asked it out loud, we both knew that we would be obliged to examine the depth of our commitment to living in the country.

"Do you want to work this hard for the rest of your life, Terry?"

The wording was so stark that I was a bit stunned. Then Mark went on to say that he was not certain he would continue to farm if it meant that our income was so marginal and the effort it took to earn it was so great. The very fact that he was questioning our choices was a statement about how far we had come in our rural development. It assumed that we *could* continue our lives this way; we had acquired enough of the skills we needed to survive. But the simple knowledge that we could survive was no longer enough for him, and he felt that the prospect of working so hard for the next decade had to promise more than a marginal financial return. In fact, we had subsidized our farm's development with money earned from nonfarm work, and each of us was losing interest in urban consulting. But the basic question addressed more than the economic possibilities — it asked about the ability of a farming life to nourish us intellectually.

I had always credited us with having moved to Maine with some real appreciation for the hard work associated with farming. By now, however, we had come to appreciate fully not only the physical rigors of the work but the limitations of a traditional farm life. That understanding had not been available to us when we had coupled farming with urban careers. It became a reality only when we adopted the daily regime of small-time farmers.

When Mark confronted me with the question, he had just completed his doctoral program and was for the first time in nine years completely free to devote himself fully to the work in Maine. At about the same time, I ended my affiliation with *Working Papers*, which was falling on hard times, and I began to do some consulting for *The Atlantic*, which had just gone through a change in ownership and was hiring new staff people. For several weeks a year, over a period of about three years, I returned to the magazine's offices in Boston. The opportunity was very fortunate, both because it gave us some additional income and because it gave me the chance — the luxury, really — to look once again at the urban life I had left behind. Now I could contrast that life with the very real experience of several seasons in Maine.

By this time, as I have described, the farm had evolved into a series of small and separate agricultural activities, each of which contributed to the overall business. We had taken a seasonal vegetable farm and expanded it into a year-round operation. On the face of it, we had every reason to feel optimistic, but despite our development, the expenses were keeping pace with the increases in our income. We were still monitoring every expenditure, justifying every purchase in terms of its practicality and its relevance to the success of the business. There was no such thing as extra, expendable income. There were no frivolous decisions about spending money and the constant pressure of having so little income and so few options to consume goods and services, at whatever level, was wearing us down. Despite our relatively modest needs for new clothes, cars, and household articles, we wanted more flexibility with our time and our income. The first years had undeniably been stimulating, but they had also been austere.

Moreover, we were becoming aware of the fact that we would need a bigger income in the years ahead because we would want to have the option of sending our son to a private high school, a financial need we had not contemplated when we moved to the country. From the moment that Jacob entered school, we heard from his teachers and from his elementary-school principal that the school system was not equipped to challenge him and that he needed both the demands of a better education and the company of more peers, which was not available in our community. Although our work had insulated us from the limitations of life in a small rural town, it had done little to protect our son from feeling lonely and different.

So both of us knew some of the answers to Mark's question. We could work very hard for many more years, but probably not without receiving a few of the rewards typically associated with hard work. It's uncomfortable to have to re-examine your choices, because it almost always means that you are about to make changes and perhaps take more risks. It was also hard for us to look critically at all the aspects of our farming, because we sensed that whatever decisions we reached would probably involve giving up some of our original goals.

It was most difficult to re-examine our commitment to raising produce and working with other farmers at the markets. From farmers' markets alone we were generating about one quarter of our 1982 income, but we were spending much more than twenty-five percent of our time on vegetable production. It was also true that the markets were never predictable outlets for crops, subject as they were to the fluctuations of weather and to customer interest over the years. The markets had had a certain novelty in their infancy, and the energy of their early years had usually attracted a strong following. But as time went by, the customers dwindled, partly because the novelty was wearing off and partly because it was simply easier to do all the weekly shopping at the local supermarkets.

The supermarket owners had quickly responded to the pressure of the farmers' markets by redesigning their produce sections to mimic the feeling of an open-air market — there were more bins of unpackaged produce, more native-grown fruits and vegetables. The supermarkets also had large budgets for competitive advertising and could offer special price advantages when crops were in large supply. We could not compete with them in a price war. Farmers' markets that had failed to educate their consumers about the advantages of freshly picked produce, or organically grown produce, were not able to hold customers intent on saving money.

Individual members of the farmers' markets also failed to respond to the challenge from the supermarkets. If we had wanted to continue to attract customers, we should have given some real thought to promotion and marketing ideas that would have continued to stimulate interest. It was no longer adequate simply to sell vegetables off the tailgates of our trucks — we needed to promote the markets, and to find some ways of developing them into more substantial and even year-round marketing centers. I think that there were real possibilities for us to locate inexpensive permanent housing within some of the abandoned inner-city buildings, where we could have expanded our marketing days and increased the selling season by setting up exchanges with farmers in different parts of the country. Mark and I tried to talk with other members about cooperative and entrepreneurial efforts we might make as a group, but we were never able to create any interest or dialogue. I think that these ideas just seemed too ambitious, too cooperative, too overwhelming for other members to consider. Our goals and the group's goals were becoming less compatible, and our disaffection with the farmers' markets began.

We did undertake one final project for the whole market, which eventually became a major focus for our own farm's growth. It began as a workshop series, a group of four weekly lectures offered free to the Lewiston-Auburn community. The series was housed in a newly developed shopping complex designed from an abandoned fire station. The interior was attractively restored and contained a good restaurant, a gourmet food store, a toy shop, a crafts gallery, and other boutiques. The second floor had a large hall where we offered the talks, and the owner of the Engine House, as it was called, underwrote the promotion and advertising of the series, which she hoped would attract customers to her new center.

Mark and I designed the workshop series, gave some of the classes ourselves, and cajoled two other members of the farmers' market into teaching with us. Most of the other market members were disdainful, and a few were openly critical. There was even one hostile confrontation with a member who announced that she was sick and tired of our ambitions for the group. I think that many saw the series as a kind of grandstanding on our part.

Community members, however, responded differently, and each of the workshops was filled with men and women who seemed interested in many aspects of horticulture and in the activities of the farmers and the market. The response to the series was not surprising to us — we had only to look around at the articles in magazines and newspapers and the reports of seed companies and nurseries to know that there was a national renaissance in backyard and community gardening. But the apparent success of the workshop series did little to persuade members of the farmers' market that we should continue our efforts to promote the group. It seemed to me that there were many opportunities available to us. We could have improved the workshop series; we could have worked with community officials in developing neighborhood gardens and projects for children and the elderly. But all of these projects would have taken an extraordinary amount of time, planning, and energy, and without any belief in their value, no one was going to get involved. And I will be the first to admit that promoting any idea, any effort, is not always enjoyable. The public aggressiveness that it takes to market made most of the farmers extremely uncomfortable. The fact that the group was made up of individuals who had chosen to live and work independently and away from urban centers should have told us something about its personality. Some of the most appealing qualities about the market members as people were precisely the qualities that made them incapable of promoting themselves. I can sympathize with anyone's shyness at having to promote his or her own interests, and to this day both Mark and I are basically uncomfortable with our need constantly to promote our farm. But I am also very aware of the fact that unless we are willing to keep up that effort, we have no hope of making a living here. Our years of involvement with farmers' markets were not encouraging.

Partly out of disappointment and partly because of the real possibility we felt we saw in gardening education, Mark and I pulled out of the farmers' markets and began to concentrate on developing our own farm in a new direction. Our first efforts were very simple. We started by collecting the names and addresses of all of our customers at the markets, and we added to that list the names of people who had attended the first workshop series at the Engine House, with a view to holding another workshop series in the future.

During these same years, we began to be approached by local granges, garden clubs, and organic farming groups to give talks on various aspects of our farm. Initially, we were very flattered to be asked, and agreed to carry our slide projector and slides of the gardens and greenhouses around to luncheons, evening meetings, and dinner talks. A little more than a decade of working the land had supplied us with enough information and amusing anecdotes to entertain our audiences. Mark's background in photography was a real bonus, because he was amassing a good collection of gardening photographs and individual plant studies. Each of us had done enough teaching so that we felt comfortable in front of an audience, and we enjoyed the response to our enthusiasm for gardening. We had no idea, however, how quickly the word gets around that free speakers are available, and we were soon giving more talks and gathering more names for our mailing list.

The second time we offered a workshop series, it was at our farm. We designed a mailing piece that announced the series and described four classes in growing vegetables, annuals, perennials, and everlastings, one subject each week for four weeks. Response to the mailing was quite good: nearly fifty people signed up for the classes, which we conducted in the farmhouse. We converted the dining room into a classroom and set up our slides and projector. We lectured, had a lengthy question-and-answer period on gardening problems, served lunch, and then encouraged everyone to spend the afternoon working in the small glass greenhouse off our kitchen.

We also used the time to promote the activities of the farm, beginning with a very conscious effort to get people to buy our seedlings, vegetables, and flowers at the farm rather than at the farmers' markets. We knew that this effort would be a gradual one, and that we would have to develop the facilities at the farm if we were going to give up marketing from the back of our truck. We also knew that it would take us several years to build up a clientele, so we systematically collected the names and addresses of everyone we met at lectures, classes, or fairs.

The following year, we decided to hold the workshop series in the fall, because we had found it difficult to develop a greenhouse business and teach at the same time. The fall series was focused exclusively on growing and designing with everlastings, and it was predicated on our own increasing interest in dried flowers and what we felt was a widespread public interest as well. We scheduled four classes and limited their size to a dozen people each. More than eighty people registered, and we spent hours on the phone and in correspondence with people, trying to schedule enough additional classes to take advantage of the response. We had clearly underestimated the interest.

The format for the classes was modeled on the first series of classes we had offered. The morning was devoted to a lecture and a question-and-answer session on basic gardening techniques that could be applied to raising dried material. We identified and talked about two or three dozen varieties of cultivated plants, and encouraged students to look for wild materials that they could gather and use. We served a simple lunch, and in the afternoon I demonstrated two projects for people to work on, making an everlasting wreath and designing an arrangement with dried flowers. We made dried materials available for these projects, and some students purchased them to work with, but we also asked people to feel free to bring their own things.

I will never forget my impressions of the students in the first two or three everlasting classes. They were women, mostly, and in many cases they had considerable experience in garden clubs, in growing, and even in arranging. On hearing the conversations that took place over coffee and tea before each class began, I quickly revised my lecture into a seminar, knowing full well that I had a class of enthusiastic and informed people.

Mark and I really liked the workshops, right from the beginning. We learned a great deal from the people who came, because many of them were devoted gardeners who came not just for the information we offered but because they simply wanted to be around other gardeners. Over the next several years, we doubled and tripled the number of classes. At first our students came from the nearby communities, then from further away; eventually, as the portion of our farm devoted to everlastings grew, people began to travel here from different parts of the country and even from Canada. Some people took the everlasting class two or three times, and it was from students that we first heard the request to offer other workshops so that they could spend another day at the farm.

There was no doubt that teaching was developing into a satisfying part of our work. Every knowledgeable student in a class stimulated us to work harder, study harder, educate ourselves more, so we could feel that our classes were worthwhile.

As the teaching aspect of our farm has grown, we have become increasingly reluctant to offer a workshop until we have had ample time to study and prepare a day that is worth the price of admission. That reluctance is shaped from our own early experience in attending seminars and colloquia offered by a variety of agencies throughout New England. When we started farming, we were hungry for information, and we signed up for day-long workshops and attended talks on land use, product development, marketing, and business skills. With few exceptions, we were greatly disappointed in the lectures and presentations. We found that the speakers were unenthusiastic, underprepared, and sometimes inaccurate. So we try to evaluate our own workshops to make certain that no one goes away feeling that he or she has wasted time. Some participants complain of just the opposite — that we give them too much information to absorb in a day. I am more comfortable with that complaint.

As the workshops became better known, we realized that we might be able to attract even more people to the farm if we could find some newspapers and magazines that would publish articles about the classes. We had begun to advertise, using a very modest budget, but there was no way that we could afford to pay for the exposure that published articles would effect. Using our knowledge of how the press works, Mark wrote letters to the editors of a number of publications, describing the classes and suggesting that the publications might want to list them in their calendars as a reader service. We attached our workshop brochures to the letters, and just as we had hoped, several editors called and inquired about the classes. There followed two major articles on the farm. The first appeared in *Down East* magazine; it was a personal profile of the two of us, and described our move from Boston and our attempts to develop a business. The second was written for *Horticulture* by a writer who attended one of the everlasting workshops and then expanded the material from the class into an article about dried flowers. We had very consciously tried to get the attention of the press, but we were very lucky, because these two articles, published in 1984 and 1985, gave us national exposure.

These days we are constantly looking for ways to make our farm visible to all forms of media, and we spend an appreciable amount of time promoting our business. I am certain that a few readers will wince at learning this, because we all sense some basic contradiction between the romantic mythology of a small farm and the more guileful world of marketing. But small farms are not exempt from any of the demands of other businesses. If it were not for our urban skills in publishing, designing, and teaching, we would have found it very difficult to devise any marketing strategies. Figuring out how to market a business has not been difficult, but the constant need to do it is the most unpleasant aspect of our work.

Mark sends out news releases about our classes, about the spring fairs, and about whatever activities we feel might make interesting reading. If one of us has the chance to give talks or go on television shows, we take advantage of it. There are many ways to get public exposure without buying advertising space. As I mentioned earlier, organizations and institutions are always looking for guest speakers, and when we became aware of this, we rather indiscriminately agreed to travel and talk about our farm and about the various aspects of our business. At a certain point we had to re-evaluate how much time we were spending on free talks, and we began to accept invitations for the audiences we were most interested in reaching and to charge a fee for speaking. Of course, this was after we felt that our presentations were valuable and we were confident that we could and needed to be paid for the work of teaching about gardening.

Having established a steady response to our classes in everlastings, we began to look for ways to expand the workshops. The next class was developed around our interest in herbs, both those that could be used as ornamentals and everlastings and those that we valued for culinary purposes. When we started growing herb plants for sale, we offered only the most common cooking herbs, such as basil, parsley, marjoram, dill, and thyme. The herbs did not sell themselves; we had to promote them, at the farmers' markets and at the farm as well. In order to do that, we had to learn more about their use, and so we began to experiment with herbs in cooking, teas, and potpourri, and we also started designing gardens with herbs. We borrowed and bought books on the subject, and discovered an area of horticulture that has fascinated gardeners for centuries.

All the time we devote to studying seems luxurious, but everything that we have studied becomes part of the material we use to interest other people in plants. Initially we offered our customers information in the form of small mimeographed pages with some botanical notations and a few simple recipes. These were a great asset in distinguishing our plants both at the farmers' markets and at the farm. By the time we offered our first herb workshop in 1984, we had enough experience in growing and cooking to present a basic introductory class, and enough customers were involved with their first herb gardens to want more information. This is just another example of the way in which the development of the farm constantly challenges us to experiment, study, and learn in order to attract customers by doing what is most interesting to us.

Our plant and seedling business evolved in much the same way. The business was founded on sales of extra amounts of the plants that we needed for our own field production. We tested the varieties, made choices we felt we could rely on, and then offered plants for sale that we felt were suited to our climate. If we had started a nursery business without being farmers ourselves, we might have made some very different choices of plants to sell. For example, you can purchase seed for many varieties of sweet green peppers at about $4 an ounce. They will germinate, and they will look like good seedlings when they go on sale, but they are almost always unsuited to the Maine soils and growing season. As farmers, we learned that we could always rely on a couple of hybrid peppers that cost $40 to $50 an ounce. Despite the cost, we naturally chose the hybrid varieties for our vegetable business, and we also chose these varieties for plant sales, because we were totally dependent not only on one-time sales but on developing a faithful clientele.

When we started selling seedlings at the farmers' markets, we offered the usual assortment of vegetables and popular bedding plants, such as marigolds, petunias, and impatiens. So did every other farmer, and so does every other nursery and garden center, not to mention some supermarkets and discount department stores. We figured that we could only stimulate plant sales by offering more unusual plants. Once we restricted our business to selling at the farm, we had to offer unusual varieties, or people simply would not make the extra effort to come. More important, neither Mark nor I was interested in producing larger and larger quantities of a few popular plants. And I suppose we rationalized our need to experiment constantly with unusual herbs, ornamentals, everlastings, and perennials by saying that we wanted to create our own niche in the plant sales business. In fact, I don't believe that we would stand a chance of developing any clientele unless we wanted to do just that. The fact that we are trying to develop a business from a remote farm in the foothills of western Maine has pressured us into looking for unusual ways to farm. Trying to solve those problems has been a large part of what captures our attention.

*   *   *

By 1984 we had withdrawn completely from the farmers' markets and concentrated all our vegetable production on the wholesale market. We hoped to replace the lost income with an increase in our wholesale vegetable sales. We had lined up a certain number of accounts that we felt were reliable: the three Arby's restaurants and about eight other, smaller restaurants located along the delivery route. If all went according to plan, we could start making deliveries early in July and continue until late in the fall. For the wholesale accounts alone, we were planting about five thousand pepper plants, one thousand tomato plants, several thousand cabbages, and smaller amounts of peas, beans, radishes, carrots, broccoli, cauliflowers, eggplants, and fresh flowers.

Twice a week we had to telephone all the restaurants to find out what they wanted, and in some cases we had to negotiate prices, since we were always being compared with the out-of-state wholesalers. Once the orders had been gathered, we had to pick, sort, wash, weigh, pack, and label the produce for delivery. Usually Mark or my father would head out early on the delivery day, with the station wagon or the truck loaded with hundreds of pounds of vegetables. The route was about one hundred thirty miles round trip, and involved anything from eight to a dozen deliveries. By the time Mark or my father returned to the farm, it was late in the day and he was absolutely exhausted. Then we had a one-day break from deliveries, during which all of us would work on other projects, such as gathering everlastings, drying herbs, teaching classes, doing book work, or dealing with customers at the shop. Then we would repeat the whole process of calling, negotiating, gathering, and hauling produce to the restaurants once again.

By making certain that we sorted our produce and delivered only the finest-quality, unblemished food, and by being absolutely reliable about delivery, despite the weather in which we might have to pick or drive, we managed to keep our accounts for a first season, and then we carried many over for a second year. We even added a few more small restaurants to our list of buyers. We did manage to replace our farmers' market income with restaurant sales, but it took a formidable amount of work to manage vegetable production along with the other activities.

In the fall of 1983, Roger had given notice that he would be leaving, and so we really felt pressed to review and possibly revise our thinking during that winter. Would we simply look for another Roger — a person who would work in the greenhouses, fields, and shop, doing everything from carpentry to designing with everlastings? For another year, at least, we wanted to continue our vegetable production. This decision was made as much by sentiment as by wisdom. We had revised our farm so much over the past several years that we were reluctant to continue changing. Neither Mark nor I was prepared to stop growing food for sale. We had developed certain skills in growing quality produce, and we also felt bound by some of our commitments to restaurant owners. We sensed too that by discontinuing our wholesale business, we would be cutting ourselves off completely from direct sales away from the farm. Our lives would then be focused entirely on work and production at the end of our discontinued road.

With those sentiments guiding our direction, we decided to hire at least one and possibly two new people for the upcoming season. That would allow us to develop the greenhouse business, maintain the vegetable production at the same level, and increase the scale of our everlasting and herb plantings and the number of products that we could design with them. We also planned to increase the number of workshops by offering summer sessions, in the hope of attracting tourists to the farm. We were becoming aware of the fact that we needed to expand our clientele beyond the state borders, in case we someday had the opportunity to market our products by mail. In addition to these plans, Mark and I had each signed a book contract, so we would need more time away from the day-to-day demands to research and write.

We placed a few ads in the newspapers and began the process of interviewing for new staff. We ended up hiring three people.

Although this meant that our labor costs would really escalate that year, we decided that we very much needed time to concentrate on marketing and writing.

All three new people began to work in April. By the end of the month, one of them had "remembered" a previous injury that would prevent him from doing the work. It was a conveniently discovered injury, occurring as it did the morning after our first day of hard physical labor in the fields. However, this man did exit early and gracefully, and we did not have to deal with the unpleasantness of letting him go. Our experience with one of the other new employees was less easy. We had failed to evaluate his ability to work hard or well, and our expectations and his were worlds apart. Tensions built over the summer, ending in harsh feelings and disappointment on both sides. The third person was delightful, and we hoped that he would stay on to become involved in farming and teaching. But that fall he was offered a position with the National Audubon Society, and left to build his career in an area for which he had studied and worked.

By the end of the season, then, we were right back to square one. Would we hire new people for the next season and go through the difficult and demanding process of training them to work with plants, deal with restaurant accounts, and wait on customers at the farm? Our figures told us that we had generated only a little more from selling vegetables wholesale than we had paid out in wages. But there had been the constant demands of a larger staff, of training, and of the administration and paperwork that are associated with a larger business. We were discouraged with the efforts it had taken to get through the season, and we were a little wary of interviewing again, knowing that we might have learned something from experience but that we would have to invest a lot of energy in starting over.

Our doubts about looking for, hiring, and training new people also begged a larger issue, and that was whether or not we really wanted to continue raising vegetables for a living. We had now spent more than a decade learning about the varieties that grew well in our climate. We had increased our yields and could probably continue to improve on them. We understood the cycles of production and could anticipate the retail and wholesale demands of our area. We felt certain that we would not want to market vegetables on a larger scale, because we could do so only at the expense of the other activities at the farm.

It's hard to give up something one has worked hard to learn and has come to do rather well. A few close friends forecast our withdrawal from vegetable farming before we were ready to articulate it ourselves. But in truth we were overextended, and much more interested in what we could learn and do with the other aspects of our business. Our interest was shifting away from food production and toward the growth of herbs, everlastings, and ornamental plants.

We called and wrote to all of our restaurant accounts during the winter of 1984, announcing that we would not be growing produce the next season. I think that we both felt that we were actually giving up farming; we had not really accepted the legitimacy of a flower and herb farm, and yet the last season had shown us on paper that every other aspect of the farm produced more income than growing vegetables did. If we were not going to generate the money from vegetables, then could we make a viable small business by growing and manufacturing products with everlastings and herbs? Once we could ask ourselves this question, we had pretty much established the direction for the upcoming season.

The constant need that Mark and I have to look critically at what we are doing is both essential and unsettling. Our evolving lives in the country are infinitely more demanding than the professional lives we left behind. Every decision that we must make has to take into account our individual needs and the degree to which those needs are compatible with the development of a farm that can produce satisfactory work, stimulation, and income. To the degree that we have both been able to make similar demands of the life here, we are indeed fortunate. We began coming to the farm when we were in our twenties. It is now two decades later, and we are still driven by the same ambition to learn. We try to develop a business that will satisfy that need, perhaps before all others. The adjustments that we have had to make to each other's needs have been less difficult than the adjustments we have had to face as our farm evolves.

Nowhere is this more true than in the necessity to accept the farm as the actual center for our teaching, writing, and selling. This change has transformed our home from a private and isolated spot into a place that welcomes, entertains, feeds, and courts a growing public. Whereas our discontinued road seldom saw vehicles (except those of family and friends and the postman) during the first dozen years of our occupancy, it is now traveled daily by customers we have quite purposefully tried to attract to our greenhouses, shop, and classes. When we started teaching, there simply was nowhere but the house in which to have the classes, and so for three years, until the barn *cum* shop was completed, we had to conduct workshops in our home, which probably contributed a lot to their success. People liked coming into our old farmhouse, and they enjoyed the lunches cooked and served in a family kitchen. Even when we were able to move our business out of our home, so the workshops and retailing could take place in a building some distance from the house, we still had to establish regular business hours and honor those hours by being available whenever a car drove down the road.

Obviously, then, the decision to make our farm the center of all of our activities had to take into account our ability to deal with a less private and reclusive life. The alternatives, as we saw them, included sending our produce and products out, wholesaling, and opening a shop in a community with enough population to support us. None of those options really appealed to us. Thus far, we are most comfortable living, working, and dealing with our customers primarily in one place, despite the compromises to our privacy.

Ultimately, we have answered the question that Mark asked

back in 1983, and in the process we have discovered that one of us will probably always be asking that question. It will reappear whenever we are feeling discouraged, tired, or disappointed. But we have also discovered that we are committed to farming the land, to learning, and to making our business support us. We have been made more confident by our small successes, chastened by our equal number of failures, and strengthened by our ability to adapt and change. I think we have begun to take ourselves and our goals more seriously.

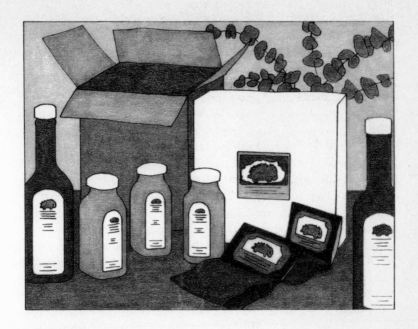

8 · THE BUSINESS OF FARMING

WHEN WE FIRST THOUGHT about moving to Maine, and for a few years after our actual arrival, we tried to make a neat distinction between our urban and rural selves. We imagined that the new skills we were learning would be more relevant to our lives than the education and attitudes we brought with us. And in fact, learning about the land, about growing vegetables, building buildings, raising animals, and becoming more self-reliant preoccupied and delighted us for a number of years.

As the farm evolved into a series of different activities, though, we began to appreciate that we were trying to define a diversified business. We also began to appreciate that we had no business or management skills, no education in financial planning, no background in the administration of a staff, and no training in product development — and our marketing efforts were simply adopted from what we had observed in our various workplaces in the city.

The distinction we had tried to make between urban and rural skills became less clear as we began to take ourselves and our goals more seriously. We realized that we would have to draw on all of our capabilities, past and present, and try to use whatever skills we had if we wanted to make our farm sustain us. We had learned to work the land, but we now had to educate ourselves in how to make a living off the land.

The work of transforming a personal undertaking into a company was difficult, and the process often made us feel quite self-conscious. That was nowhere more apparent than in our need to name the farm. Naming a special private retreat is about as difficult as naming a child. You run the gamut of names — arty, alliterative, cute, tasteful, respectably dull, embarrassing, or simply unacceptable to one or the other partner. When we were naming the farm, nothing felt right, mostly because adopting a name symbolized an uncomfortable transition. After much equivocating, we agreed to take our name from the earliest topographic maps, which called our little mountain Hedgehog Hill. The woods around here are full of porcupines, and the earliest settlers to these parts, having come primarily from Europe, used the word *hedgehog* to describe these animals. (Actually, the European hedgehog and the American porcupine are quite dissimilar in size and shape, but they both possess hundreds of sharp quills, hence the name.) There are many hills with the same name all over New England.

Around the turn of the century, spring water was discovered on our Hedgehog Hill and a bottling company was built. Like us, the company owners had to go through the process of finding a name for their business. They apparently saw the folly in trying to sell Hedgehog Hill water, so they renamed the land Mount Oxford — a solid and respectable-sounding name for a mound of land rising only eight hundred feet above sea level.

Mount Oxford was much too respectable for us, so we went back to the old name. It was a choice that turned out to be a mixed blessing. It was a great name when it came to designing our business's printed materials. I found a wonderful woodblock of a hedgehog in a seventeenth-century history of four-footed beasts, and adapted the print for our farm logo. Hedgehog Hill is, however, a lousy name for people to say or spell, and whenever someone tries to repeat it, he or she inevitably stumbles over or mispronounces it.

The day that we painted and hung our first proper sign at the end of the road, friends took pictures of us standing at either end of the sign and grinning rather sheepishly at the camera. The sign seemed so big (which it was not), so bold, so definitive as a statement of our entrance into the business world. In fact, it has taken me several years to begin not to notice the sign when I drive down our road. Apparently it struck a number of our friends that same way, because several of them commented on it, saying that they were stunned to see that we had named the farm and were actually running a business from our land. That reaction, I think, reveals some very deep-seated and romantic notions that we all hold about what farm life is all about. Those ideas preclude the need of farms to be managed, developed, and marketed according to the rules that govern every other business.

We were face to face with that need, however. Having removed ourselves from contact with customers at farmers' markets and with wholesale buyers, we had nevertheless to continue to keep in contact with a clientele for our business. We felt that our best strategy would be to use seedling and workshop catalogues, a catalogue of gifts from the farm, some selectively purchased advertising, and whatever editorial attention we could continue to attract.

We started producing a number of printed pieces each year, which led one printing company to refer to us as the publishing farmers. I guess we did look a little out of character in our overalls and mud boots, correcting galleys and page proofs in the printers' customer booth. But we were confident that using our skills in writing, photographing, and designing printed materials would be the best way to maintain contact with our clientele. We got some early support for this idea: people told us that they looked forward to the publications, and in fact sometimes quoted back some of our writing.

As I have mentioned, we methodically gathered a mailing list of customers, which grew in five years from a few hundred names to several thousand. As of this writing, the list is creeping toward the ten thousand mark. Given the fact that we have been compiling it for more than a decade and a half, I admit that our business is growing slowly, if you evaluate it from a traditional mail-order standpoint; but our names are primarily those of people with whom we have actually had some contact. We have never swelled our mailing list by buying names from other companies, as is commonly done when young businesses are starting up. It means that our growth has been slower and more deliberate, and perhaps more cautious, but it has also meant that the returns for many of our mailings have been above average. When we send out a catalogue for seedlings, we *know* that a large number of our customers are interested in purchasing plants from us, because they have done so in the past or they have personally expressed interest in doing so. When we send out catalogues on the workshops or special events at the farm, we are mailing to people who have visited in the past or who have been referred to us. Over the years we have kept records of how many pieces we have mailed and how many responses we have had, so that we can evaluate the costs of the mailing, the rate of return, and the increase in response from year to year.

From the beginning we have relied on our abilities to write material for ourselves, design our own brochures, and do our own photography — all things that we could not afford to hire. I knew how to find paper and printers, and we have our own darkroom in the cellar of the house and can prepare materials there for publication. When it came to purchasing advertising, we decided to run ads fairly frequently in only a few publications, on the assumption that we could not spend much money on newspaper advertising and would probably do better by concentrating on one audience over a period of time. I think that the approach makes sense, as we constantly hear people saying that they see our ads everywhere. That is simply not true — what they are remembering is seeing our ads repeatedly in one weekly Maine newspaper, and very occasionally in some local weeklies, which we use before the spring fair and the November open house in our farm shop.

Although the actual design and production of printed materials has not been difficult for Mark and me, the management of a small direct-mail business was at first fraught with problems and frustrations. We did not know anything about the ins and outs of the U.S. Post Office. We had to learn about buying a bulk-rate permit so that we could mail out large amounts of printed matter for less than first-class rates. We had to learn to adjust the sizes and weights of our mailing pieces so that they would fall within the limitations for the most economical postage rates. We had to learn how to label, sort, count, and weigh our mailings to comply with postal regulations. We had to learn how to phrase the mailing piece with the correct "Forwarding and Return Postage Guaranteed/Address Correction Requested" so that our mailing pieces would not simply be thrown away when we wanted address changes to keep our lists up to date.

As a consequence of all this, I strongly suggest that anyone who is starting a business try to schedule some time with a postal administrator before designing any printed material. If we had done this early on, we would have avoided a number of costly mistakes. You should ask questions about the best types of mailers for your business and the size and weight limitations, and once you have gathered as much information as possible, remember to ask the same questions again from time to time. Like most government agencies, the post office is constantly revising its regulations, and unless you ask the same questions every few months, you may find that you are designing a mailer that violates some new rules. You should also be aware of upcoming postal rate increases, so you can send out pieces a month or two earlier than you might have planned in order to take advantage of the savings.

Although Mark and I had the skills we needed to produce printed materials, we didn't have the experience to evaluate the effectiveness of some of our efforts. Our seedling and workshop catalogues were fairly well conceived and successful from the beginning. Our gift catalogue was not as well thought out. The first one that we designed, printed, and mailed offered only three different items for sale: an everlasting bouquet, an herbal wreath, and a heart-shaped arrangement of dried flowers. The cost of producing the catalogue and sending it out was barely offset by the gifts that we sold. It was not a disastrous opening gambit, but with hindsight, I realize that you cannot begin a catalogue business with only three items for sale.

The second year we increased our line of gifts by offering three times as many items — still a small number — and again we did very little more than cover the cost of putting out the publication. We tried to interpret our returns in the best way possible, by telling ourselves that even if we hadn't made any profit from the catalogue, we had kept in touch with our audience. While that is no doubt true, perhaps there were better ways to do that. It is always hard to judge the success of any piece of advertising, especially in the first years of business. We now know, however, that we need to offer a much more extensive list of products from the farm and to represent our gifts with a full-color catalogue. But in order to do that, we must develop more products that we feel are good quality, interesting, and reasonable to produce with the materials and staff that we have. They should also be products that we will want to go on manufacturing, because once they are offered in a catalogue, they should be available for a while to come.

The time that it takes to design, develop, refine, and present a new product is considerable. When we were growing vegetables for a living, adding a new item simply meant ordering seed, planting, harvesting, and filling another display box at the farmers' market. The process of adding a new product for sale in a retail shop or to wholesale buyers is not so simple. There are questions of design appeal, pricing, packaging, and the ability of the product to be shipped, and then there are questions about our ability to manufacture the product in sufficient quantities for retail, wholesale, or catalogue supply. It is quite easy now to rattle off all of these concerns, but we had to learn to define the problems of any new idea and to develop new ideas systematically. As we did, we began to appreciate the realities and constraints of a small manufacturer. Ideas come quickly; the ability to translate ideas into real products is much more difficult.

I can illustrate this most clearly by describing the development of one of our main products — the herbal wreath. As I have explained, I made my first wreath during a talk and demonstration. The farm has since sold thousands of herbal wreaths, at our shop, at craft fairs, through our gift catalogues, and in boutiques all across the United States. The story of how we moved from that first effort to producing a consistently good product by the thousands is the story of each individual item that we try to define and add to our business.

As I have pointed out, we originally made our wreaths on crimped wire frames that we fashioned by bending and shaping old coathangers. Once we began to make more and more wreaths, it was not possible to make our own frames too, so we had to find a manufacturer that produced them — and the tape and the wires and the floral picks, supplies that are necessary to produce a well-made, long-lasting wreath. In addition, we had to rethink our scale of farming to be sure that we raised enough materials to put into the wreaths. This meant reorganizing both our annual and perennial plantings and scheduling enough days in every growing season for gathering materials in the wild. If we were going to have a regular selection of wreaths available in the shop, then we had to plan ahead to have enough raw materials and enough time to design and manufacture them.

I was not able to do all of the actual manufacturing myself, and when my mother's help was not enough for us to keep up, we had to look for and train another person. That meant more money in labor costs. It also meant that we had to forecast not only the increased need for raw materials but the manufacturing needs over a year, so that the new staff person would have some definition of his or her workload and expected income for a season. We had to decide on a fair wage that was attractive enough to hold someone we had hired and spent time training. We also had to include another person at the farm, which added to our costs for workman's compensation (a legal area we had to learn about once the farm grew beyond the limits of a family workplace).

Then, with the costs of materials, supplies, and labor settled, we had to determine how much money we would charge for each wreath. This figure would have to reflect the actual costs of manufacturing plus a whole series of less obvious costs, including those parts of the farm's budget that went for advertising the product, maintaining the buildings for manufacture and selling, storing materials, and packaging, labeling, and holding the item as inventory between manufacture and selling.

The list of considerations goes on. It would be quite simple if a customer were content to drive to our shop, select an herbal wreath, and carry it out in a leftover grocery bag. Obviously, a wreath is not a pound of tomatoes, and the customer expects a box to protect it. That means that we had to hunt for manufacturers of suitable cardboard boxes. At first we chose corrugated containers for their durability. We then had to find suppliers of tissue paper for wrapping the wreaths inside the boxes. We had to design a label with the name of our company, ideally with an attractive logo and something about the wreath's design and manufacture, to take advantage of the fact that we grew our own materials and used only natural herbs and flowers in our wreaths.

Having solved the problem of how to box our wreaths safely, we were faced with the fact that our customers wanted to give the wreaths as gifts and had begun to ask whether we had anything more attractive than a brown cardboard box. It seemed a reasonable request, but it meant that we had to find a gift-box manufacturer to design wreath boxes in a couple of sizes, and we had to work with the manufacturer to figure out the specifications we needed. Then we had to figure the cost of the packaging into the cost of the herbal wreath. We also had to make certain that we always had enough boxes on hand but never had too many manufactured ahead of time, which tied up our money in the costs of the boxes and of the space to store them. The same marshaling of inventory applies to the wreaths themselves and to the supplies that go into them and the labels they carry.

Now, all of this pertains only to manufacturing wreaths for sale at the farm. Many of our customers visit us from out-of-state; they prefer to have their purchases shipped to them after they have returned home at the end of their summer vacation. Just as many customers want to send a wreath to someone as a gift, and they would like us to ship it for them. Naturally, all of the people who purchase wreaths through the mail must have their orders shipped to them, and all of our out-of-state wholesale buyers require this too, as do most of our in-state buyers. So we not only need individual wreath boxes, we need heavier shipping containers in various sizes, insulating material to protect our boxed wreaths, shipping labels, and an arrangement with a company to pick up and deliver our products. We also have to learn and abide by the rules and regulations of packaging and shipping used by the carrier.

The considerations go on. If a customer simply walks into the shop and purchases a wreath and hands me a $50 bill, I give the appropriate change (which I have to have on hand) and write up a receipt for my books and for the buyer. If the customer wants to write out a check, I have to have a policy about accepting checks. Once someone has established a retail shop, most customers expect him or her to accept at least a few of the major credit cards, and it does seem strongly to influence customers' decisions to purchase something, especially if they are traveling or on vacation. If you decide to accept any form of plastic money then you have to find a bank that is convenient to your business and that offers competitive rates for processing the credit slips. (In looking around, be careful to compare the rates, because the difference between four percent and five percent can be a considerable amount over a year.) Since Mark and I decided that taking credit cards stimulates buying, we have found a bank to handle the business and have got the proper forms to fill out and deposit (in addition to regular bank deposits).

If these endless details sound mundane, I can assure you that beginning to understand and identify them was anything but. In fact, we never quite realized that we had opened a store until we were pressed by our customers to behave like store owners. Almost every procedure and policy we have had to develop came about because one of us didn't know how to respond to a buyer's question. *Do you ship wreaths to Germany? How much would an arrangement cost if I had it done in my own antique basket? Can I have the country hat on the far table, but with one more ribbon? Will you accept my sister's check?* Mark and I stumbled and ad-libbed through answers at first, but when some of the other people on our staff were confronted with such questions, they had to ask the customer to wait just a minute while they hunted for us to help them out, which made everybody unhappy. And so, over the years, we have spruced up our products and established some procedures and policies, and still not a week goes by without a perplexing question or two. (In fact, we have saved a file folder full of wacky requests. In one case a woman asked us whether she could bring in an everlasting arrangement she had bought from another store so that we could "fix it up a little" to make it look as nice as ours. In another, a man wrote from the Midwest to ask for copies of our financial statements; he wanted to study them so he could revamp his failing nursery business into a business like ours, which he presumed took in several million dollars a year.)

After sifting through all these details simply to design, make, and sell an herbal wreath, we had to decide on a retail price for every size and variation of the wreath, and also to determine a wholesale price list. The wholesale price must be high enough to justify our time and effort in making the product, but low enough to tolerate being doubled, since most items are marked up a hundred percent by the retailers. Wholesale accounts only come back for reorders if our products sell, and in an impersonal store that sells lots of items that are not manufactured by the owners, the wreaths from our farm will not get any more attention than any other item on display. The only criterion for continuing business is the ability of the product to sell itself.

A lot of this explanation is filled with the lingo of manufacturing, pricing, selling, and packaging, because in the process of making that first wreath and trying to develop it as a product from Hedgehog Hill, we got an intensive education in the business of marketing. From the development of one product we were able to begin to ask more intelligent questions in each and every area of the herb and everlasting business, but each new product has presented a unique series of problems to be solved. Most broadly stated, we found our way into the larger world of manufacturers and suppliers.

In many cases, we simply started out with the yellow pages of big-city telephone directories, beginning as close to home as possible but sometimes ending up in Boston, New York, or Chicago. The telephone was our first access to manufacturers of bottles for our herbal honeys and vinegars, to manufacturers of ribbons for decorating our everlasting nosegays and country hats, to distributors of envelopes for packaging herbal teas and potpourris.

When it came to packaging products, we not only had to solve the problem functionally and aesthetically, we had to learn how to do it legally. Food can be bottled only in new glass. Food labeling has to be specific and complete. Packages of food and dried herbs, according to Maine regulations, must not be assembled with any harmful materials. Food items have to be stored in specific ways. All of the rules and regulations are reasonable, and they are designed to protect both manufacturer and consumer, but we had to learn what the rules were and to make certain that we were always in compliance.

Home food manufacturing is typically under the jurisdiction of the state, and each state has its own licensing process, fee structure, and inspection program. In Maine, the Department of Agriculture oversees this activity. If you are considering manufacturing products from agricultural produce, you would do well to contact your state agency first so that someone can help you plan. The direction that you will need is not unnecessarily cumbersome, but for us, at least, it was a long way from just having our produce scale checked each season at the farmers' market. Moreover, like the constantly changing rules at the post office, regulations governing food manufacturing and packaging constantly change, and it is the responsibility of the manufacturer to keep apprised of the current laws. And manufacturing food at a farm often means, as it has meant for us, that you are subject to yearly inspections by a state agent, who checks your kitchen, water quality and temperature, cooking utensils, and preparation and storage procedures. In our case, the agent has always been helpful, and she is our best source of information about suppliers, code changes, and sometimes marketing trends.

When we moved our farm business back to the farm itself, we changed our point of access to the public. Customers began coming more frequently to our land and to our buildings, and we became obliged to carry extended insurance for fire, personal liability, and product liability. The barn/shop that we designed and built is now inspected routinely for proper steps, railings, lighting, heating, water, and population usage.

Our seedling and nursery business has also grown more complex, and in our attempts to manage this part of the farm, we began to learn about yet another industry. Typically, the earliest needs in any activity are for some simple supplies and information, and the greenhouse business was no exception. In order to grow thousands of plants for sale, we had to know not only where to purchase seeds but where to get constant supplies of soil or soil mixes, containers, watering tools, and identifying labels for plants. Once again we had to search for suppliers in the industry, assess what materials we really needed, and figure out what effect these supplies would have on the costs of our plants. We also had to look at the existing standards of the business. If other growers typically offered plants in individual pots, in containers of six or twelve, then what would we do? What proportion of plant to container would allow the plants to develop best and at the same time allow us to grow as many plants as possible in our greenhouse space? If we were growing plants just for ourselves, then we would probably put each plant in its own container, with ample room for root development and light. However, in order to be cost-effective, each greenhouse had to be used to produce the optimum number of plants.

Like any industry, the plant business is full of traditions and marketing tricks that we had to understand and interpret for ourselves. This was perhaps most obvious in growing and selling perennial seedlings for sale as first-year plants. Most nurseries offer perennials as individual plants, or as a small number of plants, for prices far above those of the common annual vegetables and flowers. Even when there is no difference in the cost of the seeds, and when it is just as easy to seed and transplant a certain perennial as it is to grow annuals, the price of the perennial is markedly higher. This is the result not of the actual costs of materials and labor but of some perceived sense that people will not buy perennials each year, so the market will thus bear a higher asking price. Consumers have been trained to expect to pay more. In this case, we decided early on to offer flats of perennial seedlings, which no doubt caused some surprise among other growers. It also caused some surprise among our customers, because they told us repeatedly that they could not find the same plants anywhere else. Challenging the conventional wisdom in this case helped us to attract quite a few people to our farm.

We also had to evaluate this part of the farm's activity in terms of the number of people it would take to manage the work for a given period of time. Unlike the herb and everlasting business, which can occupy us in some way year-round, the seedling business is limited to a fixed time of year. Seeds are ordered anytime between late fall of the previous season and early spring of the actual selling year. Fortunately, we kept records of our orders and sales from the beginning, so that we could try to project our needs for seeds and supplies and our start-up costs in the spring. We also became aware of the hazard of crop failures at the seed companies, so we now try to order the seeds that are most critical for seedling sales and field production early. Realizing that we are so reliant on seed companies has pressed us to search for varieties that are not hybrids and to collect our own seeds when possible. If a crop becomes important to our business, then we are most comfortable with relying on our own abilities to grow and save its seeds from season to season.

This is all the more important because we decided to offer our seedlings earlier than most greenhouses by means of our spring catalogue. We have to write, produce, and mail the catalogue during the midwinter months; thus we offer plants for which we have not, in many cases, received seeds. Our customers expect to be able to receive all the plants they read about in the catalogue, and our credibility rests on our ability to deliver everything we offer. Our planning therefore has to be carefully controlled, not only for variety but for quality and quantity, so that on a given date — when the plants go on sale — we have thousands of seedlings of the appropriate kinds, developed to the right stage for sale. This calls for some analytical projection and not a modest amount of luck.

Like our other activities, our seedling and plant business is subject to a number of regulations and demands. We must be licensed to sell plants, and our plants are inspected several times a year by an entomologist from the state Department of Agriculture. We have always benefited by his visit, as he has taken a special interest in our attempts to raise greenhouse and field plants without the use of chemicals. He has taken unusual insects back to his laboratory to help us identify them. He brings us new information on the latest research into biological pest controls, and he occasionally sends us reprints of material that he thinks might be of interest.

Our experience with licensing agents and government inspectors has almost always been positive, but that has resulted from our attitude that their work is not punitive or personal. There aren't any regulations that I know of that I would not want applied to products I might buy. And the agents we have met are usually informed and sympathetic, if extremely overworked. I have heard other business owners grousing about the pressures they get from inspectors, but I am sure that the kind of relationships anyone is able to develop with the various government agents is very much governed by his or her attitudes about the nature of their work.

Throughout all of the changes on our farm, the area that has remained the least complicated is the actual field production. Perhaps this is because we have had longer to define our size and the diversity of our crops. These definitions are not fixed, but they are proportioned to the season and to the time we want to devote to the tasks of planting, cultivating, and harvesting. Each year we plan out our fields, to the point of drawing up a map before planting. We design the gardens to take into account the rotation of crops, the layout of the plants to be used in teaching, and the ease and efficiency of harvesting. We also lay them out with an overriding interest in the ultimate visual design, because we feel that we can, with not much more effort, design gardens that are beautiful places in which to study and work. The abilities that we have to understand how plants develop and to appreciate their times of flowering and fruiting and their relative sizes, shapes, and colors are perhaps some of the richest rewards of the years spent in learning.

One of my favorite tasks in the spring is to take the previous year's garden plan and a clean sheet of paper and work up a new scheme for planting. I sketch out ideas, trying to juxtapose textures and colors while putting plants that need daily harvesting near the fronts of the rows, leaving those that can develop for fall harvest at the far ends. I try to group families of plants, separating species by a repeating pattern. For instance, the brassica row usually starts with the earliest summer cabbage, then has a colorful annual flower, then early purple cabbage, then flowers again, then the winter storage cabbage, flowers, Chinese cabbage, flowers, broccoli, flowers, cauliflower, flowers, kale, flowers, Brussels sprouts, and flowers.

It never even occurred to us when we began farming that we might want to plan the fields to be as beautiful as possible. Now I'm as interested in the design of the gardens as I am in their function and productivity. The fields are laid out like complex tapestries, and in the past few years we have made and painted small wooden signs that identify each plant by its botanical and common names. We use the signs to educate ourselves, to teach everyone on the staff, to assist us when we are giving our workshops, and to encourage visitors to use the gardens as a place to browse.

Not all parts of the organizing and management of our farm have been as enjoyable as the actual gardens. This is particularly true of bookkeeping and money management. We moved to Maine and farmed for a number of years using only our small personal checkbook. We kept records of all of our sales and purchases, but we simply stored them in desk drawers or in file cabinets until midwinter, when Mark had to pull all of the information together to prepare the tax forms. He usually procrastinated as long as possible and then hauled out all the papers, sorted them, and tried to assign them to categories of farm and personal expenses. The work was tedious and time-consuming. We read what we could find about itemizing expenses, capital investments, and depreciating purchases, in an attempt to report our income accurately and still pay no more in taxes than was necessary. We called our accountant in Boston with questions, some of which he could answer, but he was unfamiliar with many of the questions about the business we were now in.

The bookkeeping became increasingly cumbersome. We were taking in more and more money, but our expenses for supplies, equipment, building, wages, insurance, advertising, state and government taxes, and workman's compensation were growing too. Our methods of bookkeeping in no way reflected the complexity of our business, and we had to learn to collect and organize data that we could analyze to make better decisions as well as to report our income accurately.

Our small checkbook was abandoned in favor of a one-write bookkeeping system. The largest print on our checks was no longer our names but the name of the farm. All income and expenses are recorded and then broken out into the appropriate columns for accounting purposes. When we are disciplined — or rather, when Mark is disciplined — we work up a spread sheet every month, so we can review our financial picture and compare it with the previous year's situation.

Although teaching ourselves about and making ourselves work with a more complex bookkeeping system has not been exactly exciting, the information we have been able to glean from the work has turned out to be essential. We can see how much money we have spent each season on each part of the farming enterprise. We can evaluate our cash flow from month to month. We can project what our wages might be for the upcoming season, and we can factor in a percentage increase in certain recurring costs. We are actually able to project income from the various activities more closely, and to interpret that information as we decide what aspects of the business we want to maintain, what aspects we want to develop, and what aspects we might consider abandoning. And as the record keeping improves, we are actually able to rely on our interpretations of the figures to plan budgets for an upcoming season.

I recall a seminar I attended years ago, on using computers in small businesses. The lecturer made one salient point: people buy computers not because they think they might need one, but because they want the software to do the work they are already finding too cumbersome to do manually. Almost every aspect of our farm work mandated our buying a computer as a tool, and, as I mentioned earlier, when we purchased one, it quickly became as essential to our daily operations as the tractor and the telephone. It also became one more thing that we had to learn to understand and use.

I have come reluctantly into the twenty-first century when it comes to accepting modern technology. Mark was the moving force in getting the computer, and although we have been using it for the past couple of years, I still am reluctant to struggle with any commands beyond my needs to write articles, brochures, and letters. And yet I am the first to admit that the capabilities that it gives us are invaluable. We store all of our plant information, our mailing lists, and labels for the brochures we send out every year. All of our bookkeeping is done with a spreadsheet program. We send out computer-generated letters regularly to our wholesale accounts. We even use the machine's printers to design and print simple labels for products when we are trying out new ideas and are not yet ready to commit ourselves to spending money for outside printing.

As I consider all of these areas of concern, I realize that they have been uncommonly stimulating. I never expected our rural adventure to be so broad an education. And if I turn that realization around, I also have to reflect on the way in which we have evolved the farm into a place where the stimulus for involvement is the constant need to learn.

There is another component of our rural education that we are only beginning to appreciate as the work here becomes more elaborate. We came out of the city with a strong determination to make a life for ourselves in the country, but we peopled that life with other participants, and in the process created a tiny little institution that ultimately is formed and influenced by all of the people who join in. We could have kept the farm no larger than a family unit, and I am certain that the economic possibilities for its survival would be the same if its size and directions had been limited. Mark and I really expanded our notions of this place to include the energies and ideas of other people, and in the process we have shaped and have been shaped by their needs and agendas.

To date more than two dozen other personalities have fitted somehow into this composite. They have ranged in age from fifteen to seventy. There have been more or less equal numbers of men and women. Most of our employees were born in this country, but there have also been some from Asia, South America, and Europe. And each one of the people who has come, for anywhere from two weeks to five years, has come for a slightly different reason. Some came because it was the most convenient place to work for the summer — it was near home, offered competitive wages, and was a reasonably pleasant environment. Some came because they were frustrated by what they saw as the lack of other job possibilities in the nearby communities. Some came because the nature of the work — horticulture, organic farming, and land use — was of real interest to them. Some came expecting to stay for a few weeks and stayed on for years; some came with high expectations and failed to like the place. Some came with no expectations, and found themselves really engaged in and loyal to the work and goals. I could list as many reasons for coming, staying, and leaving as there are people to talk about. What is harder to define, and what Mark and I will always be learning about, is the complex interrelationships that exist between employers and employees.

Regardless of how little or how long people have worked here, we have always grown to depend on them, whether simply to show up and perform a series of tasks relatively well or to carry a significantly heavier load. Some on the staff have taken on part of the administrative responsibilities; some have been

creative, strong with ideas and products. Regardless of their contributions, everyone has had to learn to work together, to share
some of the tasks, and to become interdependent. Every con-
ceivable human response gets played out in the fields and in the
shop: friendship, anger, empathy, jealousy, distrust, betrayal, affection. And just as in every institution, regardless of the size, it
is up to those in charge to figure out when we should disregard
the personal issues, when we should intervene, when we should
change someone's job description to accommodate everyone's
needs.

We have had to make the decision to give someone the opportunity to grow in his or her job, knowing full well that someone else on the staff will immediately feel threatened by the
change. We have had to be critical of work and at the same time
be encouraging. There is no area of the business that is more
difficult than the management of the people who work here, and
I wish I could say that there were suppliers and manufacturers
and tools to make the job easier. This is the area in which we
constantly have to rely on our insights, experience, and ability
to understand the issues. Mark and I compare our reactions, and
we play devil's advocate with each other's interpretations. We
argue about when and how to intervene in a situation, and we
try to trust our instincts when we agree that we probably ought
to let things play themselves out, that our intervention will probably not solve the problem.

Another major question has to be posed, over and above all the
specific details of daily functions and interactions with other
people. It has to do with the kind of business we want to develop
and the scale we want for that business. The answers to this
question probably come closest to defining the personalities of
everyone involved. I want to make a living off the land, but I am
not interested in reorganizing my business or my way of life for
the purpose of making money.

There are two examples that I can offer to try to clarify my view. Since we opened the retail shop at the farm, and since we sent out our first gift catalogue, we have been approached by dozens of people with products that they would like us to consider including in our business. A number of these items have been well conceived and manufactured; no doubt they would sell, and they would offer us the opportunity of expanding our shop and catalogue rather quickly. On reflection, though, I'm not interested in being a shopkeeper. I very much want to develop ideas and products from the work that goes on *here*, because they come from a context that I am deeply attached to. Even though the growth will be slow, it will be an integral part of our farm.

We have also been approached by many catalogue companies and wholesale agents who want to include our products in their catalogues or in their company lines. The prospect of having a very large farm, where we would manufacture and wholesale large quantities of products and where Mark and I would end up supervising more people and more production, is equally unattractive. I moved to the country to work the land, to learn more about the skills of rural life, and even though we have evolved the farm beyond my original notions of what it would be, we do not want to change the nature of our business so completely that we are no longer doing the work we find so compelling.

Living on the farm continues to be a rural adventure, but only because it takes shape from things grown out of the soil. On a good day, the sun shines, everyone gets along, the UPS delivery person arrives on time, and there are enough customers in our shop to cover the costs of making the products and offering them for sale. If it's a really good day, Mark and I agree about what it is we hope to accomplish, and the day ends with a feeling that we have come close.

On an acceptable day, there is a shower or two, we don't quite get as many plants transplanted as we wanted, and the tractor is firing on only three cylinders, so someone has to check the wiring.

On a typical day, some customer praises our fields for their beauty, two people on the staff are barely speaking to each other for reasons we are not certain we understand, and I have forgotten to order supplies for the wreath makers, who need more wire frames before they can continue to work.

We are still farmers, and yet we have moved awkwardly and reluctantly into the world of business. We are trying to juggle many conflicting demands and find a balance that allows us to preserve our dreams of a rural life. But all things considered, for the time being at least, there is no other place I would rather be.

9 · RURAL BONDS

I AM BEGINNING to know why I am here, and why I want to stay. For the efforts I have made, I have chosen the rewards that are most important. Foremost, my work and my pleasure are one and the same thing. I can make fewer and fewer distinctions between what I must do to make a living and what I want to do with my time. There are few places that I want to leave this place for. This very ordinary piece of land has become my home, my office, my laboratory, and on it I am able to work, play, study, and live, all the while enjoying an environment that is so beautiful, so stimulating, and so seductive that I have become unfit to live elsewhere.

As the years have passed, I have come to need less and less of the approbation that comes from seeing my name on letterheads, on mastheads, or in association with others whose esteem helps guarantee my own. I also care less and less about the security of my position, knowing full well that as my rural knowledge and skills increase, my marketable skills disappear. At some time — a few months ago, or perhaps a few years ago — I turned a corner, and I am probably unemployable in the traditional sense. That doesn't mean that I couldn't once again make my way into the traditional workplace. It really means that I no longer want to, and that I hope I have the wit and instinct to avoid it.

If this sounds smug, I don't mean to. What I mean to say is that I've struck upon a place and a set of tasks that fill me with wonder, fascination, and the promise of a lifetime of interesting work. Most probably I will never retire from all aspects of what I now do, and yet at the same time I trust there are many permutations to come. If I cannot make the whole place fully understandable, perhaps I can write about some of its parts, and as the description unravels, we will both have a better understanding of what binds me here.

There is no day when I am not struck by the richness of my environment: the visual beauty, the qualities of light and air, a sense of space, and the interplay of quiet and sounds that are predominantly produced by the natural world. I always walk to work. Most often I head out across the lawn of our house, either right or left around the gravel turnaround to the dirt road that leads to the entrance to the main garden, the greenhouses, and our shop. It is a journey that I make several times a day, back and forth to the farmhouse for lunch and a few other errands. The distance is only four hundred feet in one direction, but it will take more than my lifetime to begin to appreciate what takes place in that space.

It is winter as I write this. The walk is icy at the moment, because we have had several days of snow, sleet, and freezing rain, which has compacted and hardened what little snow there was on the ground. The town plows our road just to the turnaround, and we have to hire a neighbor to clear out the rest of the space for vehicles and machinery. That leaves us about one hundred feet that we have to keep shoveled — paths to our house and to the shop. Daily traffic on the paths has eroded the snow down to the bare ground, and the recent sleet has left them as glistening strips of ice, impossible to maneuver unless we spread ashes from our woodstoves and furnaces on them.

I always resent having to plow the snow into mounds so that we can live and conduct business at the end of this road. I wish that we could dismiss the need to park cars and deal with customers. But that is a conflict that I will always feel, as long as we continue to have our farm and our business on the same site. So on my daily walks back and forth, I try to disregard the manmade mounds, the manmade paths, and let my eyes be entertained by the other sights of the winter landscape.

There is still enough snow to cover the ground completely, but not enough to obliterate the clear delineation of garden rows, both in the perennial flower gardens by the house and in the main production garden in front of the shop. The conformation of the snow cover does more to exaggerate the shape of the raised beds than the actual plantings in the summer do. The land rises and falls, and each raised ribbon of snow is decorated with the debris of last year's garden. The garden in winter is its own reward for leaving everything unplowed until the following spring. There is every imaginable variety of color in the plants, which are dead and decaying, dried and wintering over, evergreen and dormant until the warmth of the spring releases them into new growth.

The first row that I see as I enter the main garden contains the remains of oriental vegetables, some of which are very tall and have thousands of seed pods that will produce volunteers in the April ground. The mustards are the most striking winter forms in this row. Their long cylindrical seed pods are nearly all opened and curled back — nature's efficient way of distributing next season's population.

The next thing that catches my eye is the row of ornamental grasses, nearly all beige, bleached by the sun to tones ranging from honey-colored to dull off-white. The birds have been feeding from the millet seed heads. I harvested the largest heads, which we marked off with string so that they would not be picked for everlasting arrangements. That left a few unharvested stems for food, and I noticed that the birds came later to our house feeders this year, probably in part because of the abundant food left in the garden. In addition to the millet, there were ripe amaranth and teasel, not to mention several hundred varieties of vegetables, herbs, and flowers that produced seeds.

I always take several walks through the winter garden. Depending on what time of the winter I'm there, these walks serve a number of purposes. Early in the season, I am reminded of the garden's recently ended splendor. The sun and storms have not yet had time to erase all of the color of plants killed by the October frosts. The zinnias and asters still retain a faded color, and even some blossoms are held frozen by the early winter temperatures. The snapdragons are still green, reminding me that in a slightly warmer zone they truly are perennials. Their greenness once fooled me into thinking that they were going to survive our Zone 4 winters, which they seemed to do until the alternate freezing and thawing of spring did them in.

One of my favorite spots to visit in winter is the section of ground devoted to the cole crops — the brassica family of cabbage, broccoli, cauliflower, kale, and Brussels sprouts. After we have harvested all that we will use, there is still plenty of food left on the plants. The cabbages that were harvested early have usually sprouted several small secondary heads. The broccoli has gone on branching long after we have picked and frozen a winter's supply, and there are usually a few Brussels sprouts and lots of kale left for gathering.

The gleaners start coming late in October and early in November. They always come after dark, as they are wary of the human smells that we have left in the garden. We see their tracks in the mulch of the garden rows, their hoofprints where they have broken through the black plastic row covers, and finally their clear traces after the first snow covering. I always hope for snow after the end of the hunting season, because deer paths are so easy to sight in the snow. The number of tracks that I saw for the first time a few weeks ago told me that at least a few of our visitors had survived the November hunting season to return for their nocturnal meals.

Winter is actually the best season in which to appreciate the size of a homestead. The leaves are gone, and the snow cover reflects light through forests that would otherwise be visually impenetrable because of leaf cover or sheer darkness. Perhaps it is my delight in the sense of being able to see for such distance that compensates for having to live in a climate that has gray, denuded trees for fully half the year. (I remember the first time I actually counted how long the trees were leafed out and how long they were bare, to realize that ratio. A long time indeed to live in a landscape that seems not to be living.)

If I don't care to see the effects of snow removal, I need only to leave our farmhouse from the kitchen door on the east. I travel that path every day as well, for it is the direction that takes me over the lawn to the back pasture and the horse barn. Every morning and late afternoon, the animals need to be fed, watered, cleaned, and let in and out of their stalls. We have had horses for only a year now; they are our first real indulgence since our move. We bought the first one late last fall as a birthday present for Jacob. We knew as much about horses as we did about gardening when we started, and it is great good fortune that brought us a six-year-old gelding named Redigo, a breed horse, part Pasofino, part American saddlebred, and part Welsh pony.

The idea to buy our son a horse was so quickly agreed on that we had only a month in which to build a temporary winter shelter before the horse arrived. We bluffed Jacob into thinking that we were building a tool shed in the field behind the house, and he grudgingly agreed to help us, all the time wondering why we needed yet another outbuilding and wishing that he didn't have to help in its construction. On his birthday, a car and horse van drove down our road, and we sent Jacob out "to see if it was a customer for the shop." The passenger in the car, rehearsed earlier by us, asked whether he was Jacob Silber, and when he replied that he was, she said, "Good, we've got something here for you." She and the driver got out of the car, opened the door of the van, walked Redigo out, and handed the lead rope to our son.

This was one of the moments we will remember and talk about for the rest of our lives. Jacob was stunned, disbelieving, thrilled, and a little intimidated by the size of his birthday present. In fact, we were all a little intimidated when the former owner and her friend left. Here we were with about nine hundred pounds of young, excited, frightened horseflesh. Furthermore, we had not yet had time to finish the shelter, so one of us — Mark, of course — had to climb on Redigo's back (without benefit of a saddle) and ride him about six miles to a neighbor's farm where we could board him for the three days and nights it took us to finish our carpentry.

Redigo was young and only moderately well trained, and he had just been taken from his lifetime home, a stall right next to his father. Mark had been on a horse about a dozen times in his life, each time on an older, trail-riding horse and in a big Western saddle complete with pommel. When he began the ride to our neighbor's barn, it was already dusk. I followed along behind him in the car, trying to stay far enough back so that I would not spook the horse and yet close enough to rush to Mark's aid if he was dropped off unexpectedly. The procession went smoothly until we got about a mile down the road and had to pass the first farm that had horses of its own. Redigo caught the scent of the other animals and began to call out. He was quickly answered, and that convinced him that he was going no further with a rider. I would definitely have lost courage at that moment, but Mark held his own, and there ensued a rather tense contest of nerves and will, the horse intent on making a right-hand detour and the rider intent on continuing the journey up the road. Fortunately, Mark convinced Redigo to continue. He didn't have to pass any other farms with animals, and we arrived an hour or so later at the Abbott farm, where we bedded down the animal and asked Stewart Abbott as many questions as we could think of (very few, in fact, since one has to have at least some knowledge in order to form questions). Then we returned home.

In the next three days we finished our building, bought hay and grain, and put up a fence around a small pasture outside the building. Once again Mark coaxed our new horse away from other animals and down the hill to his new home. I remember specifically asking Stewart Abbott how we would know whether the animal was all right — whether there was a problem or he was ill. The answer was that we would know. Indeed, that turned out to be right.

On one of the coldest December days of that first winter, Redigo came down with colic, a common but serious illness in horses, caused in this case by a change in diet. Mark went out to the barn before I did that morning, and came back to the house to ask me to come with him, because he thought Redigo was acting strange. He was indeed. He hung his head, dragged his legs, and kept trying to lie down and roll over. We called the vet and were told that she would be on her way as soon as possible, but that it sounded like colic, and the horse would try repeatedly to roll over to reduce his stomach cramps. We should do all we could to prevent him from thrashing about, as he could effectively strangle himself on his seventy feet of intestines.

We had by that time read enough about horses to know that colic can be a serious, even fatal illness, so we spent several frightened hours walking our animal around the turnaround and up and down the road, in an attempt to keep him from rolling on the ground. The vet came, examined and medicated the horse, and told us that we would have to watch and wait for the next twenty-four hours before anything else could be done. We took sleeping bags into the barn that night. It was about five degrees above zero. Redigo was in real discomfort, and it was also impossible to keep him from rolling over and over. We rubbed him, talked to him, tried to comfort and distract him, and at about one in the morning he began to quiet down a little. He thrashed less and groaned less, and actually slept for fifteen minutes to a half-hour between pains. We were so frozen that we went into the house to warm up and sleep for a couple of hours ourselves. By morning the horse was definitely on the mend; we were exhausted but extremely relieved. We felt that we had passed a kind of initiation, and at that point we began to believe that we would learn something about horses and that we could trust our instincts in dealing with animals.

We looked for several weeks this past fall for another horse. This time we could at least ask some reasonable questions of the prospective sellers. We began to see differences in the overall conformation of types of horses, and in the temperaments of individual horses. We are coming to understand the term *a kind eye, a good eye.* Sundance is our newest horse; she is an eleven-year-old American quarterhorse. We took her along with her stablemate, a young Alpine goat. We hadn't ever considered having a goat, but we felt that the move would be easier for the horse if she were accompanied by an animal she was close to. So here we are with a gelding, a mare, and a goat.

Jacob, Mark, and I have been taking riding lessons for about half a year now. Jacob is easily the best rider. He sits well in the saddle, walks, trots, and canters adeptly, and is always on the correct diagonal. Mark and I are responding more slowly to the instructions, but we are beginning to know a little. I can walk into a tack shop now and recognize what I'm there to find, or, if I am not certain, I can use some horseman's vocabulary to get help. This is a familiar route. I recognize that I know very little this year, but I am also certain that I will have much more information and understanding in the years to come. This is the beginning of another adventure. With time, experience, reading, and observing, I will gain a kind of literacy that I don't now have. The daily walk to and from the horse barn is just one in a series of lessons.

*   *   *

Three sides of the horse pasture are bordered by very old stone walls, undoubtedly built in the youth of this farm, because they mark off some of the fields closest to the farmhouse and thus must have contained the first spaces for growing crops and maintaining animals. One of the walls runs southeasterly from a corner field near the house, up the long incline to Hedgehog Hill, and along for a distance of some five hundred yards until it meets another, equally old wall that divides fields from the pine plantation. I've walked along this wall countless times, climbing slowly until I reach the end of the field, where I can sit and look out over hills and valleys that are miles away. Aged stone walls make me feel very secure, and not a little insignificant. The rocks have grown dark with repeated exposure to the seasons, and they often wear coverings of lichens and mosses that only years of neglect will allow. One can build a new stone wall with some skill, but no one can manage the color or patterning of stones that seasons and time will produce.

Each time I walk up the hill (or each time I walk anywhere in nature), I am always torn between the urge to discover every small bit of adventure that is taking place on the ground before my footsteps and the desire to watch the larger, more dramatic unfolding of landscape and form that I can see if I keep my gaze fixed higher. The ways in which a person walks and looks around seem to be attached to different emotional states. Eyes kept downward keep the thoughts busy and close, jumping from small patterns of insects and plant life to personal and private turmoils. When you remember to lift the head up, you are usually forced to stretch out your observations and to reflect on shapes and meanings in a broader context.

When I'm troubled, I usually walk to the far stone wall, turning over the details of a mood, conscious that my walk is tense and aware of the impact of my feet as they hit the earth. When I reach the wall, by habit I head for a particular spot where the stones form a series of natural benches for sitting. My eyes are usually still focused on the minutia of the land immediately before me. The process of working out my thoughts and tensions is accompanied by an increase in the distance of my gazing, and the journey out of conflict is always assisted by the same visual relationships. I gaze down the field to the farmhouse, seemingly small and insignificant, and then over the house and its maples, also dwarfed by the distance, and I begin to notice the familiar shapes of the mountains and valleys in the distance. Sky and clouds and light move over the horizon, and inevitably I forget myself for a moment. I can count on this exercise to help release tension, even if all the details of my life remain the same, and even though I never attempt any great answers. When I retrace my steps to the house, my gaze invariably wanders from the ground at my feet to the larger landscape, and I am less aware of the impact of my feet on the ground. I don't need to understand the mechanisms at work. I do need to know that the land will always release me from a claustrophobic vision. There was never any exercise in the city that I could count on for the same refreshment. I knew of activities that could divert my attention, like going out to a concert or movie or, better still, going shopping, but activities like these usually rebounded, and once they were over, deeper dissatisfactions crept into my thoughts.

The stone walls connecting the upper field to the front field run through a variety of smaller climates, including a section of wetland that supports a vigorous stand of alders, pussy willows, blue flags, jack-in-the-pulpits, sweet flags, and winterberries. In this little area I am constantly made aware of life's smaller struggles. The wall is filled with chipmunks, mice, and moles, and the wetland bushes are the nesting sites for a variety of birds. When Jacob was younger, he spent a considerable amount of his time in the swamp, sliding and skating there in the winter, smashing rocks through the soft spring ice, watching for the first frogs' eggs and pollywogs, then catching frogs and snakes throughout the summer.

Our cats like to hang out in this little zone as well. Their motives are less playful. Sadie, the one-eyed part-Siamese we brought up from Boston, can sit motionless for long stretches of time right at the break in the stone wall that marks the entrance to the garden. We usually know when she is there, because the chipmunks are scolding. But inevitably she claims her prize and displays for us a maimed animal, which she then plays with until there is no life left. The end of the sport is evidenced only by an abandoned tail. My gut response is still to try to catch her before she has broken the neck of her prey, and to seize the chipmunk or mouse from her jaws. My head tells me that the felines of the world will not survive if this one is not allowed to keep her instincts honed. Still, this is one of the spectacles that I try to avoid watching on my walk to work.

But there is another spectacle that is far more cruel, if one is keeping score of nature's little games. It involves the annual spring cycle of frogs that come out of the ground to sing, mate, and lay eggs in the standing water of the small swamp. We always look for the first gelatinous green egg masses, which swell with time and release thousands of pollywogs into the water. All goes well at first: the pollywogs grow, their heads begin to size up, and their legs start to grow. At just about that time each year, the swamp begins to dry up. The water level drops daily, and thousands of partly developed frogs are forced into a smaller and smaller puddle. When the swamp is reduced to a tiny puddle, it is nothing but an area of writhing mud, and then the robins and snakes move in for a great feast. About a day or so after the swamp has been cleaned and abandoned, there is usually a rainy period, and water is replenished to the level it was at before the frogs went through all of their labors.

The first year that I watched this happen, I was horrified, and I panicked. I gathered several large plastic buckets, filled them with water, and tried to scoop up the pollywogs so that I could relocate them in a nearby pond. I don't try to save them all anymore, but usually some new person on the staff goes through the same frenzied attempt, and I am struck with a tender feeling for the newcomer and the effort.

I forgot to include snakes among the inhabitants of the stone walls. They may be the most abundant species there. We see hundreds of snakes during any given season — almost always garter snakes, ranging in size from the six-inch-long youngsters to the more mature specimens, approaching two feet in length. My mother made very certain that I would be afraid of snakes; so profound was her own fear that not only could she not hide it, she felt urged to promote it. My grandfather also feared and hated snakes, and because my father said that he wasn't afraid of them, he was often sent out to frighten them away or to kill them if they were too near our home. I am waging an active campaign to rid myself of my inheritance. Cleo has been the biggest help.

I don't any longer remember how we came up with her (his?) name, but one summer, many seasons ago, we repeatedly saw a small garter snake curled in the sun just at the entrance to our main garden. She seemed uncommonly unafraid of our comings and goings, and eventually I actually looked forward to seeing her and would stop and study the intricate patterns of color that played up and down the sides of her body. If one of us got too close, she would slither off into the swamp, but usually at a slower-than-usual pace, which I didn't recoil from so strongly (it is the rapid slithering of snakes that usually startles me). One morning we found her unusually docile, and realized that she was burdened by a bulge about two inches back from her mouth: she was in the process of digesting what was most likely a frog or a toad. I realized that she was quite vulnerable at that point and yet had exposed herself to all our traffic. We were getting used to each other. I never saw her or any snake quite like her after that year, but I continue to be met on that part of the road by any number of snakes making their way from one side to the other. They are usually moving rapidly, and they always increase their speed as footsteps approach.

The garden itself is filled with snakes, especially since we began our complete mulching system. The black plastic is a perfect hiding place for them, and they slither in and out of the holes that we make for planting, feeding on the insects and frogs and toads that also live there. In the early part of each season, I am always startled to come on them while I'm working in the soil. By midseason I am more relaxed with their presence, and by late summer I can detect the very subtle but distinct sound of their movements beneath the plastic, which are usually invisible to the human eye because of the vegetative cover. The only time we see them clearly is when they cross a garden row, rustling across the dry hay mulch.

One of the real luxuries of gardening in Maine is that we don't have to worry about poisonous snakes, and knowing that, Mark and I have attempted to help Jacob enjoy and handle these harmless creatures. One of the most beguiling species we have ever come across is a very small, pistachio-green snake, which we hardly recognized at first because its color camouflaged it perfectly in the garden. When Mark picked it up to show it to Jacob, it reacted by spitting out a glistening red tongue in great contrast to its body. I've only seen this kind of snake a couple of times, but the color is so delicious and the size so small that my first reaction is pleasure rather than alarm — some small progress in my attempts to unlearn fear.

Perhaps the most common and dramatic urban response to the rural experience is demonstrated by people's reactions to insects, especially to the numbers and varieties that everyone encounters nearly every season here. I am most aware of it now when our urban and suburban friends and family visit the farm. If an insect lands on a person, or on a countertop or a window, the first instinct is to slap, to grab a paper and swat, or to get up from the chair and step on it. I've even been told by someone across the room that there is an ant near me; implicit in the information is an instruction to kill it. I must have felt that way too when we first came. I've lost track of the changes in my attitudes; they were so slow to take shape, and so imperceptible.

I do remember when I first came to realize that there were

categories of beneficial, as opposed to harmful, insects, and that I should never kill ladybugs, lacewings, and praying mantids. On the other hand, I have seen more than one devastating infestation of Colorado potato beetles, Mexican bean beatles, aphids, and flea beetles. I've also worked to the end of my tolerance in those early planting days that coincide with the arrival of the blackflies. And when I've really wanted to garden during the lovely cool summer hours of dusk, just as the mosquitoes are ready for dinner, I've been driven into the farmhouse. But for the infinitesimal number of insects that I can categorize into the good-guy or bad-guy role, there are thousands about which I remain unclear.

If I were to assess insects by their visual appeal, then I would assign great virtue to the Japanese beetle and probably always destroy a syrphid fly, thinking that I was under attack by a wasp. And we have neighbors who are amateur beekeepers and who bring hives to our farm for the summer. We have seen wild swarms of honeybees in the last few years, and I actually helped one beekeeper remove a lumpen swarm of bees from the top of our fir, so he could bring it home to add to his collection. I can't describe what a thrill it was to handle a branch covered with thousands of clustered bees without feeling the least bit afraid.

So if I don't know who the good guys are and who the bad guys are, and if I feel more wonder than fear, how can I be expected to understand the command to kill an ant on my kitchen floor? This can become a problem when you extend the sentiment to household cleaning. Thus far, I compromise: I clean up cobwebs without destroying the spiders, especially the small spider and its progeny that have lived for a couple of seasons now between the kitchen-table lamp and the little herbal wreath on the wall right above it.

If this confession of my eccentricity has you wondering, you may give me a reprieve when I tell you that I have tried to overlook the spring influx of houseflies, and the sudden onslaught of houseflies in the bedroom that we close off for the winter, with no success. After numerous attempts to shoo them out the open windows, I usually resort to a frenzy of vacuuming them up, feeling all the time that I really have lost perspective. For the time being, however, the ants can come and go with the seasons, and the spiders and hornets are still allowed in the house. Any houseguests who want them dead are going to have to carry out their own executions. But I'm saddened to see such an immediate and unthinking desire to kill insects, because it reveals a basic feeling of alienation from other living things.

There is perhaps nothing that distinguishes the urban from the rural environment so much as the smells. For the most part, I summarize the city as a composite of manufactured fragrances. Industrial exhausts, smoke, and automobile fumes pervade the outside air, but the air in buildings is even more of an assault, perhaps because I am aware of how many attempts are being made to mask animal scents. Cleaning agents, industrial and personal deodorants, colognes, perfumes, and fragrances manufactured into clothes, furniture, plastics and paper all compete to create a uniquely nonbiological potpourri. The rules for living in the city are quite clear: manufactured scents are altogether acceptable, human scents are not.

It would be devastating if we could mask the smells of life in the country, not because they are all pleasing, but because they all help us to form deep attachments to people, activities, seasons, and places. I know the smell of my house, because nearly a hundred and fifty years of life have gone on here. The smell of the dirt floors of the cellar combines with the odors that wood laths and old plaster have absorbed from wood fires, kerosene lamps, cooking foods, and human sweat. On damp spring days when it is still too cool to open the windows and doors but warm enough to release the layers of smells, I am reminded that whatever we do to this house, we will only contribute our share to the history of scents that define its personality. We have reconstructed rooms, torn down walls, sanded floors, papered, painted, upholstered furniture, but the smells of this old house have been only slightly altered by our tinkering.

On my daily walk to work, I am as conscious of the smells as of the visual details. In winter the cold is mixed with the down-draft of smoke from the woodstoves. Our woolen sweaters and jackets, hats and mittens carry the smells of the fires, the kitchen, and especially the horses, if we have recently worn the clothes into the barn. When we cut and haul wood for the house and greenhouses, we have the smell of mixed woods, the pine most fragrant, the oak strangely musky.

In spring there begins a real competition of fragrances. Melting snows and rains release the smells of rotting duff, mud, and new vegetative growth. Ironically, one of the first flowers to bloom in our area is commonly called stinking Benjamin (it is better known as trillium or wake-robin). Its slightly rotten smell allows it to compete for the attention of flies, who are attracted to its carrionlike aroma. The weather is not yet warm enough for all the insects that pollinate the sweeter-smelling flowers like lilacs, mock orange, narcissus, and lily of the valley.

When the competition for insect pollination is in full swing, the fruit trees, berry plants, and flowering trees and shrubs are all doing their part to scent the early summer air. At this time of year, it is not so much individual smells that one is aware of as the richly fragrant air — some days dry and warm, some days moist and heavy, but always provocative. We are in the fields for the longest hours at this time, working the soil, cleaning gardens of their mulch, weeding, planting, and transplanting. The smells that I have grown to recognize and anticipate from season to season have become as reliable as maps, calendars, and watches. I rely on them to reassure me, with all of the other stimuli, that it is early May, that it is early morning, that I am by the back door, and that lilacs are wonderful this spring because they are here and so am I.

We are also spreading animal manures at this time of year, as are most other vegetable and dairy farmers in our area. When I first came to the country, I automatically held my nose when we drove past barns that were being cleaned out or fields that were being manured. I made no distinction between the smells of cow, horse, pig, chicken, and even human excrement. My response was conditioned to the association rather than to an actual interpretation of the smells themselves. I have since been in countless barns, have raised most farm animals, and have built and moved our own outhouses. It still seems a little embarrassing to extol the virtues of the smell of a cow or horse barn as compared with the smell of a chicken barn. But I do now make those differentiations. And I have to remind myself to keep special boots for working in the horse barn and never to wear those boots into our shop when customers are there or, worse still, when I run errands in town. Just the other day, a good friend got into our car and noted that both Mark and I carried the smell of our horse barn. We smiled a little sheepishly, remembering our own reactions when neighbors first visited us with their barn boots on.

The country air of late summer evenings carries the most intoxicating aromas. There are some nights when the basils and salvias are so fragrant that we can detect them from hundreds of yards away. I walk through the gardens nearly every evening in mid- to late summer, hours after the workday has formally finished but usually minutes before the last daylight. My footsteps release the dry, sweet smell of the hay mulch, and as I brush against the different plants, I often do not need to see where I am to know what is next to me: dill, fennel, basil, mint, salvia, marigold, tomato, yarrow, artemisia, mustard, lavender, scented geranium. Leaving the garden, I pass areas of lush undergrowth in the wetland area, walk past the conifers at the edge of the lawn, go up over the grass and through the artemisia and phlox near the porch. The upper field is full of lavender and mints at this time of year, along with artemisias, and it is bordered with huge oaks. I reach the uppermost stone wall and once again sit on moss-covered rocks. The mosses, having been heated by the day's sunlight, give off a slight fragrance that is both sweet and dank — almost a metallic smell. If I step over the wall into the pine forest, particularly after several days of rain, the mushrooms have sprouted, and the smell always takes me back to my girlhood days at Girl Scout camp in a pine forest on a lake shore. Inevitably, I am reminded of the odors of the damp canvas tents and the stale cot mattresses stained with the urine of little girls who were away from home for the first time.

Fall, like spring, is a mixture of the fragrances of things in full health and things dying, especially after the first hard frosts. Annuals recently killed by frost hold onto their smells for a while, then they begin to smell like decaying vegetation. Even the heavily scented perennials and herbs begin to lose their scent as the weather grows colder and the days shorter, and the prevalent smells in the air are those of decay, firewood being cut, and even gas from the chain saw. I'm not certain that I can differentiate between the feel and the smell of coldness, the feel and the smell of dryness. They are how my nose recognizes winter once again.

In the most literal sense, it is always stimulating to work outdoors. It is also often pleasant. It is sometimes annoying, and occasionally even stressful. I think that people usually have to confront themselves when the work is primarily physical, to recognize the level of their stamina, strength, and capacity for discomfort. Even in the most idyllic circumstances, when the temperature is comfortable, the sun is shining, and the task is moderately pleasant, a worker still has to measure his or her capacity to repeat the tedious tasks that are associated with farming. Throughout many of these tasks, I am often torn between the desire to stop working when I reach a certain point of fatigue and the wish to finish the task so I can be free to do the next job.

I've learned to work way past my interest in the particular job at hand. I've learned to find a working tempo that is repetitive and long-lasting. I've learned to disregard time and physical progress when I am performing a task, so the awareness of the ratio of work done to work ahead does not overwhelm me. I've learned to consider the agenda for a day and to disregard the agenda for a week, for the same reason. I've learned to work beyond the feeling of exhaustion, of extreme physical discomfort, to reach a point of real satisfaction in endurance. Each time I am able to get beyond a certain plateau in attitude or exertion, I am fed by the satisfaction of that achievement. The game of pushing, stretching, compensating, enduring is a constant personal test, as it is for any worker. Developing the ability to work extremely hard for long periods of time can become addictive, so much so that my years of farming have left me with the opposite challenge: how not to be working, how to relax, how to be unproductive. I suppose the pleasure I experience in working hard physically is similar to the thrill people get from running, although I doubt that I will ever have the time or the need for recreational exercise.

In retrospect, the first winter that we lived here was very uncomfortable. We were often not quite warm enough. As the snows deepened, it took more and more effort to cut and haul wood. Similarly, farming vegetables for season after season was something akin to being in training for an athletic endurance event. We walked miles and miles every day, bending, squatting, lifting, carrying, beating our bodies into shape so much that there was something hypnotic about the work, far beyond its capacity to sustain us economically.

There is no weather in which we will not work outdoors, and no weather for which we have not learned to prepare ourselves physically. I know that it is important to wear natural fibers because of their abilities to breathe in air and to retain warmth. I know that I must have footgear that protects my feet and ankles, and that keeps me dry when I have to spend several hours planting in the driving rain. I know that when I head out for a day of work in the cold, I must be layered, so that when my body heats up and the sun grows warm, my lack of preparation doesn't aggravate the discomfort or fatigue of the work itself.

I know the feeling of summer heat, when the temperature

reaches into the nineties by one o'clock and the sun picks at skin that has already been weathered by weeks of exposure. And I've worked through the discomfort of having to do my share of the work, miserable in my sweaty, dirty clothing, while the men strip down to the minimum. I've actually ranted with anger that women cannot work shirtless in the summer heat, so resentful have I felt at having to cover myself when others can bare their chests and backs to the fresh air.

There have also been, over the years, an endless number of days when the work we have set out to accomplish has been so engaging, so engrossing, that we forget to pace ourselves, and the day ends long before we want to stop to rest and eat. There have been days when I have been angry at the shortness of time, when I couldn't wait until the next morning to get back to work. There have been days when I could measure no accomplishment but still felt fatigue. There have been planting days when I have seen a piece of land transformed from an unmanaged tangle into a beautiful garden. We have cut and hauled and piled brush and trees and watched a new field take shape. We have also watched areas be reclaimed by overgrowth, when we have failed to find time to maintain projects.

I've held a baby bird, nursed a butterfly back to health, and torn my hands on machinery. I've napped on three-inch-thick moss carpets that cover the granite outcroppings on the top of Hedgehog Hill, and I've lost nights of sleep because I injured my back lifting bushels of potatoes. I've walked barefoot over newly seeded rows of clover and bruised my legs and feet building stone walls. One day I was so hot and miserable that I ate lunch sitting in the middle of the Nezinscot River, fully clothed. Other days I've been so chilled and wet that it has taken hours to warm up again, and when I have, I've felt a burning sensation in my face, hands, and feet. I've seen a blue-violet sky with a double rainbow so vivid that I was for a moment frightened. I've smelled that sweet, sickly, warm air that can foretell the coming of a severe thunderstorm, often accompanied by hail. Two years ago, just such a storm devastated many of our crops, and lightning set our house on fire. I fought alongside friends and neighbors to save our home from burning to the ground, and I fought unsuccessfully to save a neighbor's house.

Mark and I have indeed defined for ourselves an agrarian life, albeit not in the way we first imagined. We have been stunned by the degree to which the undertaking has led us into areas of concern that we did not anticipate. We have worked very hard to make a business out of farming, and I'm never frightened anymore about our ability to take care of ourselves off this piece of land. That confidence has not always been there. As recently as five or six years ago, I was sometimes startled, often without warning, by the realization of the risks we were taking, the trade-offs we were making. Note taking, data analysis, projections of our plantings, workshops, and seedling sales are all valid ways of trying to understand an upcoming season, but all of these efforts can easily be rendered inaccurate by factors well beyond our control. The real reason I am no longer afraid of the struggles ahead, whatever they might be, is that in the process of learning to survive in the country, I have formed a deep bond — not to the house or the business or the community, but to the land itself. With or without the efforts that we make, the land will continue to yield its annual and perennial crops of plants and animals by the billions. All of the agriculture that we undertake is our way of imposing our aesthetic, our order, on a small space for the time that we are stewards here.

10 · AN ENCYCLOPEDIA OF THE WORLD

IT IS CURIOUS to me that we have come to define our lives here as completely agricultural. We could have developed a relationship with this place that would have allowed us to live here and work elsewhere. Mark might have pursued his work in anthropology or in teaching. I considered and refused an offer to continue my career in publishing. We could have gone on using our Maine farmhouse as a retreat and devoted ourselves to enjoying its natural environment. If we had never seeded or planted one thing in our lifetime, this land would have done quite well with its own biological agenda. Our interest in plants and animals could have been directed to learning about the thousands of species that are indigenous to this homestead.

Obviously, I cannot answer all the whys and what-ifs, but I strongly suspect that our choices have been heavily influenced by the history of this place. We bought a house and a piece of land, but we inherited a rich agrarian past.

Years before we came, the original forests on the property were cut over repeatedly. It is rare to find a tree much more than forty years old on our woodland, except for the plantation set out in the late twenties. The only other trees of any scale are the ones that were left along the stone walls and the great old maples that shade and ornament the lawn around the farmhouse. When we came here, the fields, once used for raising crops and cattle, were beginning to disappear again into young forests, and without our interference they would just be further along in their cycle.

It's fascinating to watch the pattern of growth in a field that isn't mowed for several seasons. All over our homestead, the process follows a predictable cycle. First the grasses are invaded by other weedy growth and brambles. Then sumac and poplars start to grow, followed by alders and willows if the land is wet. Next come the small pines, the birches, some maples, and then ash. We once cleared an old field behind the house, but then didn't have the time or money to remove the stumps and mow the piece. In only five years the woody growth was more than ten feet tall, and we had to cut and burn all over again before we could have someone bulldoze to prepare the area for pasture.

Although the barns on this farm had been allowed to deteriorate and collapse, we were able to salvage a number of old tools out of them, including hoes, shovels, rakes, hand cultivators, seeders, sickles, scythes, wooden hay rakes, and a horse-drawn double-bladed plow. Only a short distance from the house, abandoned apple trees struggled through hundreds of suckering branches to produce edible fruit. Unattended brambles bore berries, and asparagus beds that were quite conceivably over a hundred years old sprouted faithfully every spring. But our most abundant inheritance of plant life from this land's previous owners was its flowering shrubs, perennials, and herbs.

As I noted early in this book, our introduction to agriculture really began with an abandoned flower garden tucked into the corner of the south lawn. The garden included achillea, veronica, tansy, vinca, forsythia, dianthus, columbine, and roses. This assortment is an interesting mix of forms, colors, flowering shapes, and sizes, but for someone like myself, perhaps the most interesting information was hidden in the very names of the plants.

I'm certain that I first came to know achillea by one of its common names, yarrow. The word *yarrow* is a corruption of the Anglo-Saxon word for the plant, *gearwe*, and the Dutch word, *yerw*. But there are endless other common names for this plant, including milfoil, old man's pepper, soldier's woundwort, knight's milfoil, *herba militaris*, thousand weed, nose bleed, carpenter's weed, bloodwort, staunchweed, sanguinary, devil's nettle, devil's plaything, and bad man's plaything. Those are the common English names I've come across in my reading, and one can assume that there are countless more in as many other languages, since yarrow was brought to this continent originally from Europe and Asia.

Luckily, some time ago an international language was developed for talking about plants and animals, and we are primarily indebted now to the Swedish botanist Carolus Linnaeus, who worked in the late eighteenth century to bring into usage a binomial system of nomenclature for all living organisms. To refresh my memory, I went back to my college botany texts and reviewed the units of plant classification — groupings called kingdom, phylum, subphylum, class, subclass, order, family, genus, and species. The binomial system is based on the last two units, the genus and species, which give a plant its scientific name. This means that people all over the world have a way of communicating about the plants they all see growing in their gardens.

Mark and I were prompted to teach ourselves the universal language of plants early on, so that we could exchange information with his parents. His mother had studied and taught agronomy in Russia; his father had grown up in a family that owned and operated a large lumber business in the Carpathian mountains of Poland. The only language that allowed us to communicate about the crops in our fields and the trees on our land was the botanical terminology.

Scientific names of plants are derived principally from Latin and Greek. There now exist international congresses for regulating these names, but biologists have always needed to invent names for new plants as they have been identified, and the history of naming plants is rich and intricate. Sometimes the names have actually been adopted from the Greek or Latin vocabulary, but many have been chosen to honor some distinguished scientist or public figure. Just as frequently, names refer to mythological characters, or they are derived from some physical characteristics of the plants themselves.

Let's get back to the common yarrow. Its botanical name turns out to be *Achillea millefolium*, words that are both mythological and descriptive. It is said that Achilles used this plant to staunch the wounds of his soldiers during the Trojan War. (Ancient herbalists referred to it as *herba militaris*, the military herb.) When I discovered its botannical name, I had a wonderful excuse to go back and reread Bulfinch and Hamilton and to simplify the story of Achilles for Jacob, who was about eight at the time, and eager to hear any story that had to do with wars and soldiers and great escapades. I was also able to interest him in the species name, *millefolium*, when he was beginning to study the metric system; the name is derived from the plant's many-segmented foliage, and has the same prefix, *mille*, as the metric measurements for thousands. I began to be grateful to whoever had included yarrow in our old garden. Not only did we have flowers to enjoy, we began to have a great deal of fun researching information about the plants.

I read in an old herbal that yarrow was one of the more commonly used herbs, both for divination of spells and as a medical preparation, and out of these various usages came its endless series of popular names. As a snuff it was called poor man's pepper. As a tea it was used to treat several illnesses, the most common one being colds. I found this history fascinating, if a little archaic. Then we were visited one day by an older woman who was a member of a Catholic order of nuns in Canada. She asked whether she could buy some yarrow plants to grow in her garden, since the order still used yarrow teas for any bronchial trouble.

Thus one plant, simple in shape, color, and form, gradually became a treasury of information, stimulating beyond any other study I had undertaken. Learning the names of other plants has also provided me with some amusing excursions. I had entirely forgotten what I was taught in high school about Latin phonetics, so I hauled out various references to help clarify the correct pronunciation of words that are sometimes Latin in origin but more often are Latinized. I found that the various books, encyclopedias, and catalogues are not consistent in their phonetic guides. I also found that Mark, with his background in Slavic languages, I with my background in English, and one of our staff members with a background in Spanish all had slightly different ways of pronouncing the same words. Apparently we had encountered an old problem, because I came across a pertinent anecdote in a wonderful book called *Botanical Latin* by British scholar and writer William Stern. In his introduction to pronunciation, he writes: "Botanical Latin is essentially a written language, but the scientific names of plants often occur in speech. How they are pronounced really matters little, provided they sound pleasant and are understood by all concerned."

Stern then goes on to describe how Erasmus, noticing the lack of uniformity in pronunciation, published a book in which

he described how a French ambassador at the court of the Emperor Maximilian made a speech in Latin "with so Gallic an accent that the Italians present thought he was speaking French"; a German, called upon to reply, sounded as if he was speaking German; "a Dane who spoke third might have been a Scotchman, so marvellously did he reproduce the pronunciation of Scotland" . . . Nevertheless, people were able to make themselves understood.

The author points out that in English-speaking countries, there are two main systems for pronouncing botanical Latin, the traditional English pronunciation used by gardeners and botanists and the academic pronunciation adopted by scholars. All of this gives me ample reassurance, and enough latitude to enjoy all of our interpretations, just so long as we understand one another.

The books that concern themselves with names, Latin pronunciation, ancient herbal practices, and mythology have all begun to provide me with other richnesses of living in the country. An interest in plants is the common thread that connects the physical pleasures of gardening with a reading list that borrows from the life sciences, history, mythology, language, and of course literature itself.

Veronica was one of the first plants that I lifted out of its tangled bed and relocated in a circular garden that Mark and I painstakingly dug out of our rough lawn. The garden measures about nine feet in diameter and is edged with three rows of used bricks, salvaged from some of the chimneys we tore down. The botanical name for the plant we have is *Veronica spicata*. Plant literature says that the genus name comes from Saint Veronica, who is said to have wiped Christ's face on his way to the Crucifixion. The species name describes the shape of the flowering part of the plant. Our inherited veronica is a clear blue, and we have since brought in both rose and white varieties of the same species. It is a hardy perennial in our climate, and can be propagated by division or from seeds. This information all seems so simple now because the plant has become my own. But not long ago at all I was trying to wade through the names, habits, and attributes of endless lists of plants.

I was initially impatient with my ignorance. I devised a number of schemes for trying to learn the common and botanical names, for trying to remember which plants were perennial, annual, and biennial. I tried to remember the sizes and heights of individual species, the colors of bloom, the time of bloom, the methods of propagation. I used three-by-five cards, cut out pictures from seed catalogues, and constantly returned to the books when I couldn't remember whether a plant was hardy or not in our location.

Gardening is not for the impatient, and as I learned this information year by year, I came to realize that everything begins to fit into place only after you have involved yourself with each and every plant. Recently I came across a cut-out picture of veronica, caught in the pages of a reference book. Now I can't imagine not knowing that the plant is hardy here, that it spreads rather rapidly in a garden, that it has the most graceful blue spiky flowers, which come into bloom late in June and go on flowering well into the summer, or flower a second time if the earliest blossoms are removed. It also attracts more bees than any other plant we have, including the bee balm. It is one of my favorite flowers for cutting. No wonder it was included in that small space by a gardener before me. It is as familiar to me now as anyone with whom I have been in constant contact for nearly twenty years. So are hundreds and hundreds of other plants. The time seems to have gone quickly, and I wonder now at my initial struggles to make sense out of it all.

Tansy, *Tanacetum vulgare*, which is one of our favorite everlastings, is thought to have been named from the Greek word *athanatos*, meaning immortality. *Vulgare* is a frequent species name, because it simply means common or wild; tansy grows wild all over Europe and Asia. When women first settled in America, they typically brought supplies of seeds of their favorite plants with them, in envelopes or containers or sewn into the hems of their skirts. They were particularly careful to include seeds of the plants that they used for household medicines, as women were responsible for preparing simple remedies to attend to the needs of their families. The English make a Lenten dish known as tansied eggs, which I would recommend only if you are curious, because the dish is strangely bitter and not very pleasing. But tansied eggs were supposed to purify the body after the sparsity of the Lenten diet. Tansy was also believed to increase a woman's fertility if applied externally and to cause abortions when consumed.

Tansy is referred to in the older herbals as a strewing herb, which means that it was strewn over the floors of houses and churches for its fragrance, in this case to repel insects. I've placed branches around the kitchen when the ants first invade the house in spring, and the insects do indeed withdraw from the plants. I've seldom seen tansy attacked by insects in our garden, either, but on one excursion to gather some plants in the wild, I saw some tansy that was thoroughly diseased.

This brings to mind some interesting questions about plant populations and disease. The tansy in our gardens grows among hundreds of other varieties of flowering plants, many of which flower at the same time and many of which are similar in color. The diseased tansy that we found in the wild was almost the only yellow-flowering species in a three- to four-acre gravel pit. This one species had colonized so heavily that the whole area was a brilliant golden yellow when seen from a distance. What a convenient and exposed target that species was for the disease or insect that caused the damage.

Conventional farming — monoculture — similarly sets up easy targets for disease and predation. It is no wonder that single crops planted year after year on the same pieces of land become prone to disease and must be protected by the constant manipulation of chemicals. Agriculture is an unnatural attempt by humans to control exact growth in a given space. As growers, we try to disregard the fact that without the interference, any piece of land would foster a very complex evolution of plant species that respond to the conditions of the soil and alter it by their growth and decay. On any untended piece of ground, different species of plants develop over time. Seeds are introduced constantly by animals and weather conditions. As species grow and change, the composition of the soil is affected, and plant life competes for space, nourishment, and light. In a field, for example, as grasses give way to woody shrubs, which in turn give way to soft woods and then to hardwoods, the competition for space and light allows some species to tower over and effectively suffocate other species. When the crowns of the trees dominate the area, new undergrowth begins to establish itself in the increasingly acid soil that is formed by the decaying leaves and needles.

When we had our first garden, the field had been lying fallow for a number of years. The botanical life of that field was in constant synchrony with the conditions of the soils, climate, and animal predation in the area. When we interrupted that cycle, we began to make considerable demands on that soil. We wanted the maximum number of plants to grow, flower, and fruit. We also wanted the plants to be free of insects and diseases, but we were introducing hundreds of species into a manipulated environment in the hope that we could coax these plants into producing.

There are many entrenched attitudes about ways in which to cultivate the land successfully. Those attitudes are formed by habit, prejudice, experience, and personal expectations. I would strongly urge any gardener to examine the alternatives carefully before deciding how to use the land and what to expect the garden to provide.

Our first garden was planted under the guidance of neighboring truck farmers, as I've described. Their answer to weed problems was to use herbicides. Their answer to diseases was to use chemical sprays. Their answer to predation was to use guns and traps. From the beginning I knew that my responses were going to be different. If I had been convinced that these were the only ways in which to garden, even on the family scale, I undoubtedly would have remained only a weekend visitor to this homestead. I can say emphatically that they are not the only ways, and I watch the proof of that position take place every season.

Alternatives to conventional farming techniques are difficult, time-consuming, and sometimes discouraging. To date, organic farming can probably best be managed on small-scale, diversified operations. Admittedly, there are crops with which we have had only limited success, and I am quite willing to forego growing them for commercial use. Apples are an example: our trees show some damage from scale and fungus, but that is decreasing as we pay more attention to careful pruning, mowing, feeding, and cleaning (when we find the time). The apples are perfectly acceptable for our use. They are much more than acceptable in that they are totally free of chemical residues. Sweet corn is another example; it has been troublesome to grow on a large scale. We seldom get more than one picking of our corn before the raccoons move in. We have problems on some of our vegetables and ornamental plants with the tarnished plant bug, and since I am unaware of an effective biological spray, we choose to accept the losses of some of our crops.

On balance, however, the successes far outweigh the failures, and each season there is more evidence to encourage our attempts to farm without chemicals. Our gardens are designed to be very complex and constantly changing. This makes them interesting places in which to work and study, but it also makes them less subject to widespread disease, because most diseases and insects attack only specific plants, and we simply have too many host plants for these problems to have a significant impact on the whole garden. We are also prepared to accept some losses each season, and our experience tells us that some years are beneficial to certain plants, which will perhaps respond less successfully to cultivation the following summer. We can avoid problems by constantly paying attention, by isolating diseased plants when they appear, by using biological sprays such as pyrethrum and rotenone on a limited basis. We can prepare plants to withstand field stress by hardening them off and by mulching them to prevent dry soil and competition from weeds. These methods are working for us. By that, I mean to say that we are satisfied with the quality and quantity of our harvests in the context of using the land without poisoning it.

Our community has endless examples of land that has been tilled and abused for decades. In fact, there is a field adjacent to ours that is, geologically speaking, the same field as the one we are using; the only distinction is ownership, marked by the stone wall behind our shop. We farm on one side of the stone wall, and have for sixteen years. Our soil is still a rich chocolate brown. It has been given ample feedings of manure, lime, and compost, and we have taken care to keep heavy machinery from compacting it. Until recently, the field on the other side of the wall was also farmed for many years, probably longer than ours. I have never seen manure, compost, or lime added to the soil. It was traditionally plowed every fall, then the soil was left to blow away with the winds or wash away with the rains. The land is actually depressed where the rows were planted each year, because so much soil has been removed from the spot. The farmer abandoned the field because he grew too old to farm it, but the deadness of the soil would have driven him from it anyhow. Even in the spring the soil is powdery, anemic, light in color. There is not an earthworm to be seen on this field. We tried unsuccessfully for three years to use this piece of land, but our best efforts to grow food on the plot were thwarted because the land had been so abused. It will take many years to bring this piece back to health. I don't know how many seasons it will take to cleanse the land of its chemical poisons, for it was farmed when people were less discriminating in the federal certification and the application of chemicals than they are today.

Not too many weeks ago, a woman who had attended several workshops at our farm called to ask for some advice on starting plants in her new greenhouse. As we talked, I could tell that she was weighing my advice against the advice she had been given by a garden-center owner. She was hesitant to use chemicals, but she didn't want to start all those seeds and then lose everything to disease. Her questions betrayed her real anxiety about growing perfect plants without problems. Should she make her own soil mix or buy prepackaged sterile mixtures? Should she drench her seed flats with fungicides? What would she do if she got damping-off disease in some of her flats? These are very reasonable concerns, and since my livelihood depends on having successes, I understood them. She went on to tell me that the garden-store owner had told her that she could not possibly grow plants in a greenhouse without using sprays and fungicides. If we didn't use them at our farm, then perhaps I could assure her that she wouldn't have any problems?

My answer was no, I could not, because gardening without chemicals involves taking a number of risks. It means being willing to accept some initial losses, until you develop the eye to detect plants in distress. It means gaining the experience to know when to try to nurse a plant to health and when to destroy plants before they infect their neighbors. It means that some years you are plagued by damping off, which necessitates reseeding some flats. It means learning to water on time and to use the right amounts, so you do not promote superficial root growth at the expense of healthy deep root systems. It means having to wait out days and days of overcast weather that does not provide adequate light for young plants, days when you cannot open the vents in the greenhouse to let in fresh air.

I could not give my caller the assurance she wanted. I could sense her growing anxiety over the phone, as she kept repeating the warnings of the garden-center owner. In the end, all I could suggest was that she examine her own attitudes and values and make the decisions that coincided with how she wanted to garden and what she expected from that experience. But I hoped very much that she would choose to take the risks and accept the failures of gardening without chemicals. If she is willing to take that as her point of departure, her experience should teach her how to adapt her techniques, and there is a growing body of literature that she can call on to educate herself.

When it comes to gardening with ornamental plants, one of the best encyclopedias or guides to plants that will succeed in a given area is free and available to anyone who is willing to spend some time exploring the meadows and gardens around him or her. For example, the vinca that I mentioned finding in our abandoned garden can be found all over this part of the state. Vinca is a spreading, low-growing ground cover. It puts down new roots constantly from each of its nodes, and effectively suppresses its competition. It runs profusely along roadsides, in old cemeteries, along the foundations of abandoned homesteads. You also see it in well-cultivated gardens. Furthermore, I have never witnessed any disease or insect damage on the leaves or the flowers of this plant.

Vinca minor, commonly known as periwinkle, takes its botanical name from the Latin word vincio, meaning to bind. There are at least a couple of interpretations of the meaning. One source states that the plant's long trailing stems were used for tying and binding. Another source states that the name is a description of the plant's growing habit, which seems more likely.

References to vinca in literature, folklore, and herbal history are numerous. I am particularly curious about one report of interest in the plant by pharmacologists in the early 1920s. Apparently it was thought to have some chemical properties that could be used in the treatment of diabetes. This is coincident with its historical use as an herbal medicine. I need to reserve some time to go to the library and look up references to current research with medicinal plants.

Having expressed that curiosity, I hasten to add that it is purely an academic interest; I would not want to recommend plants that can be used to concoct homemade remedies. I have absolutely no doubt that there are endless benefits to be derived from plants' medicinal properties, but I have enormous doubts about the increasing number of self-proclaimed herbalists, businesses that make great claims for herb-based diets, and all other forms of hucksterism in the name of "natural remedies." If we were to believe all of the literature that exists on medicinal herbs, we would have to be wary of any individual's ability to discriminate between the true chemical properties of plants and the properties that have been assigned to them on the basis of their form, color, use in astrological literature, use in pagan ritual, and on and on.

One very interesting example of this is something called the doctrine of signatures, which was popular for about a hundred years during the mid-sixteenth to mid-seventeenth century. This doctrine set forth a theory that there was a correlation between the appearance of a plant and the appearance of the disease or bodily organ that it was supposed to cure. For example, the perennial lungwort, often grown for its ornamental spotted leaves, took its common name and its botanical name, *Pulmonaria officinalis*, from the belief that the plant resembled the diseased lung; hence it was said to contain medicinal properties for healing lung disorders. Numbers of herbalists added to the doctrine of signatures, but according to my reading, one of its strongest supporters was an Italian philosopher, Gianbattista della Porta, who added a goodly number of imagined plant origins and medicinal uses. What fun it would be to make these associations! Any gardener could immediately think up some clever uses for plants.

I began to use our vinca for more common purposes, in an attempt to design a wreath from the plant's beautiful evergreen leaves, which resemble small laurel leaves. I decorated the wreath for the holidays with winterberries and bittersweet, and the leaves responded so well to being worked with, and they retained their shape and color for so long, that I knew that they must have made their way into ornamental crafts long before I came upon them. Indeed, research into the history of vinca taught me that the plant was employed by many ancient societies for creating garlands, to commemorate both the living and the dead. Perhaps because of its delicate scale, it was woven into wreaths to be placed on the biers of children. Further reading revealed that the plant appears very frequently in literature — in Chaucer, Wordsworth, Rousseau, and Bacon, to mention a few.

Another plant that we inherited, dianthus, also appears frequently in literature, although often under its more common names. The genus name comes from a combination of two Greek words: *dios*, meaning God, and *anthos*, meaning flower. God's flower is exceedingly fragrant, and we know it by the common name sweet William. Dianthus is a large genus, containing more than three hundred species of mostly ornamental plants, includ-

ing carnations and garden pinks. We inherited an extremely fragrant and unshowy variety of sweet William that keeps cropping
up all over our farm, not only where we have transplanted it but
where winds and birds have distributed the seeds. My early familiarity with these plants encouraged me to order other species,
and as a beginning gardener I wanted the biggest, boldest, show-
iest offerings in the plant catalogues.

In fact, most of the first flowers that we ordered were showy
plants. I was attracted by promises of early blooms, big blooms,
bright colors, long-blooming varieties. My initial gardening tastes
were almost entirely determined by the flower alone, and I dis-
regarded other parts of the plant. I was fairly unaware of the
beauty and importance of foliage. I was grateful if the plants were
fragrant, but only if they had showy flowers as well. At first I
wanted annuals that would bloom all season long, and I even
remember being disappointed with perennials of short season.

You only have to study the seed catalogues to know that my
response was all too common. The greatest number of pages are
devoted to petunias, marigolds, zinnias, impatiens, and geraniums. There is constant work in plant hybridization and manipulation to produce yet another double-ruffled, larger-than-life,
flat-to-frost-blooming whatchamacallit. Some of the most common bedding plants in American catalogues are vulgar in their
coloring and totally disproportionate in the relationship of their
foliage to their flowering parts. When I visited a nursery center
several months ago to examine different species of shrubbery,
the salesperson who came out to answer my questions tried to
convince me of the merits of a particular rhododendron by saying
that its flowers were as intense as the colors on a black-light
poster. I just shook my head and walked on. He thought that he
had impressed me with his sales pitch. I was disgusted that we
want plants that are in such poor taste.

But I haven't forgotten how obvious my first gardens were. I
am just beginning to know the pleasures of seeing gardens as
more complex forms. We designed a new garden last year, and

although we used flowering plants, we chose them primarily for the subtlety of their flowers and the beauty of their foliage. One section is planted with about fifty long-spurred columbines, but only the white and yellow varieties that bloom in the early summer. When their blossoms are spent, the plants are very quiet and graceful clumps of scalloped leaves. The garden includes bloodroot (a very short-season bloomer), hosta of various kinds, white flowering astilbe, and yucca. All of these plants are interwoven with a variety of ferns and low-growing ground covers. It is a partially shaded garden, meandering in and around some selectively chosen ash, maple, and butternut trees. I love the garden for its quietness, especially as the dappled light moves about over its differing forms and shapes. I even love the garden when it is past its prime, because I can watch the plants becoming dormant or withering down to disappear into their roots until the next season. The more I garden, the more I begin to appreciate each and every plant in its broadest context.

It's time again to go out into the winter garden and steal a few branches of forsythia. It is my way of hurrying spring along. Forsythia is fairly easy to force into bloom by placing some well-budded branches into a container of water and then letting them sit in a sunny window for anywhere from one to three weeks. The branches will begin to take up the water and the buds will develop so that soon you have a bouquet of the yellow flowers, long before their natural flowering time in May.

Forsythia is an interesting bush, presenting its flowers before its leaves. This farm must have had five or six old plants — judging by their size, well over fifty years old. About five years ago we carefully lifted one of them and planted it out in an open spot on the west lawn. It now stands about six feet tall and has an even larger circumference. Since we have done very little pruning, except what was necessary to trim broken or winter-injured branches, the shrub has developed its own graceful spreading shape.

While an elderly gentleman was visiting our farm last summer, I overheard him comment to his wife that it was such a treat to see a forsythia left to assume its natural size and shape. This man had spent his working life as a plantsman and greenhouse owner, and his remark made me reflect on the way that shrubs are typically used around American homes. Foundation plants, property dividers, and hedges along walkways are all common in landscaping. Most of the time, these plantings are as uninteresting, as unrelated to the land and the homes they are supposed to enhance, as are the omnipresent resealed blacktop driveways. Depending on the location, you can predict what shrubbery you will find — the familiar rhododendrons, azaleas, boxwood, and holly. I remember street after street in the Boston suburbs where the shrubs are variations on this theme. The plants are formally clipped and cleaned, the grass is always cut, and the clippings are gathered and carried away. These neighborhoods always seem sterile to me. Whenever you see people working in the yards, they are usually from a landscaping crew, and their purpose is to keep the grounds looking perfectly manicured. It is rare to find a home where there is a graceful blending of deciduous and evergreen shrubbery; in fact, friends living in one of these suburbs were once criticized because their vegetable garden was visible from the front of their house.

I suppose that my complaint seems spurious when so many millions of American houses sit naked on their plots of land, without even the slightest attention to trees, shrubs, or gardens. Although I read and am told that interest in gardening is on the increase all across this country, it seems that we lack the consciousness of working with plants that can be seen in many other countries. My memories of travels in England, Wales, and France are filled with pictures of gardens, both public and private, and we traveled there long ago, before our own lives were involved with horticulture, so we made no special efforts to visit well-known gardens.

Just last summer, Mark, Jacob, and I took a three-day trip to

Quebec. We drove north on Route 27 through the rural Maine towns of Stratton and Eustis, across the border at Coburn Gore, and then through the Canadian towns of Woburn and Lac Mégantic. I didn't need to go through a customs check to know that I was in a different country. The rural communities on each side of the border could not have been more dissimilar. The last Maine towns were small, based on agriculture, and impoverished-looking. Yards were often littered with pieces of machinery, buildings were often in disrepair, and there was little evidence of family vegetable or ornamental gardening. On the Canadian side of the border, the same kind of little communities were absolutely beautiful. Machinery was not visible, and the modest farmhouses and outbuildings were well maintained. But even more impressive was the evidence, in nearly every yard, of the handiwork of a gardener. There were flowerboxes, perennial and annual beds of flowers, almost always a vegetable garden, and well-maintained lawns. As we got closer and closer to Quebec, the larger villages still showed evidence of gardening everywhere. Finally, in Quebec itself, there were public gardens filled with workers reshaping flowerbeds, and every shop and every small hotel decorated its windows with windowboxes. When we retraced our journey home, we were struck again by the poverty of the Maine towns, evidenced not so much by the modest homes as by the owners' total indifference to the land around them.

There were lots of roses growing along trellises and fences in those Canadian towns, but they were not like the roses that I found in our abandoned gardens. Our roses would not be noticed by a passerby, primarily because they are so unassuming in color and form. There are four different kinds, as far as I can detect. The wild roses that bloom early in the spring run throughout the property and spread rapidly if they are not held in check by the lawnmower. Then there is a very special large-hipped variety that stays in one contained clump in the middle of the marshy land. If we can ever afford to put in a farm pond in that spot, I want to be certain to relocate that clump. The other two roses are light- and medium-pink varieties that grow in the original corner garden. They are simple-petaled and fragrant, and the blossoms last for only a couple of days each.

All of this is by way of saying that I recognize each of these plants as roses, but I am nearly totally ignorant of the more than one hundred species of plants that exist in this genus. The rose is the most popular cut flower in America. There is a society for enthusiasts, the American Rose Society, founded in 1899; its headquarters are in Columbus, Ohio, but it has an international membership nearing twenty thousand. Many people who visit our farm are surprised when they ask us about roses and we answer that we know nothing at all about them. It is not because of a lack of interest. Roses are on our agenda, but there they sit, with so many other items that I sometimes wonder when we will ever get to them. Perhaps the roses will catch the attention of some future owners of this land. Perhaps those people will lift a plant and relocate it, look up its name, research its history, and then set off on an adventure that will engage them unlike any other. And maybe they will be less concerned with the achillea or the columbine. I wish that I could meet and talk with whoever left me my corner garden. I wish that I could know that person and learn when and why he — no, most likely she — chose the plants she did. I wonder if she waited as eagerly as I do for them to come into flower. I wonder if she brought bouquets into the farmhouse early in the spring.

I wonder who else will pick these flowers, and I also wonder what will happen to this farmhouse and this piece of land. As I grow older, I begin to see Mark and myself as yet another generation of owners, and to think about the inheritance that we will pass along to Jacob. I think about it particularly in the context of what we have done to the land and what I want to survive. Most of all I want to define our goals clearly, in terms that are not a burden to our son. He knows how much we are attached to this place and how much we have worked to restore some agriculture to part of the homestead. We have also built buildings on the land, and someone will have to consider how these build-ings should be used and how to pay for maintaining them. I wonder how much of this acreage will be affordable for one family in years to come. Will the pressures of development force some-one to divide the land up into house lots? Will Jacob's children, or his children's children, even want to keep this land? Will they wander through its woods and fields to sit on stone walls that look out over the mountains and valleys?

My honest worries are not about whether the land will stay in any one family. And I really don't care whether it is maintained agriculturally at all. In fact, I don't really want or expect that, because the process of finding and reclaiming a homestead has been a very peculiar and very personal journey. The legacy of this place should rest not in the labors of any particular family that comes here but in the life that the land itself sponsors. I hope that some, if not all, parts of this land remain undeveloped. That way, I am certain that its richness will continue to lie in what anyone can discover here.

We chose to accept this land's agricultural past and to impose our particular interests and aesthetics on it while we use the space. An alternative and ongoing aesthetic is taking place with-out our interference. My particular engagement has been brought about by my involvement with some cultivated plants; I became a student of what I was working to make happen. I could have become a student of what was happening naturally. In either case, the lessons to be learned can only be available if the land is guarded and cherished. So the legacy that I want to pass on to Jacob is one of fascination with the natural world. I also dare to imagine that a few people who spend time working with us or walking across our land will share and thus help protect these same dreams.

SUGGESTED READINGS

After several attempts at picking and choosing from the hundreds of books that fill our shelves, I have put together a brief list of titles that might interest the reader. These titles range from how-to books on vegetable gardening to general horticultural reference books and books on the etymology of plant names. Depending on the subject being discussed, we rely on nearly all of these volumes to help us with the work of running this farm. Some of the books are for dipping into, some help settle arguments about how far apart to plant the Egyptian onions, and some are to be read and reread for their ideas and inspiration.

I have not included the names of any old volumes on horticulture, some of which I have mentioned in the book, because I want to direct you not to one title but to a period in the history of agriculture in this country. Books published between the mid-nineteenth century and the first third of the twentieth century are filled with information and interesting attitudes on farm and household management, and you will find many of them an engaging look at life in small rural communities. We have purchased most of our copies at rummage sales, flea markets, and used-book stores, and I can only direct you to the same sources. These rather ordinary volumes are not valued for their bindings or color plates, and so they are usually available for very little money. They will, however, bring you hours of enjoyable reading.

The following reading list is divided into three categories: a general series of titles, followed by books on herbs and then books on everlastings. As a final note to those interested in further reading, I suggest that you check any university and college libraries, any public garden and arboretum libraries, and any gardening and herb societies in your area.

Books of General Interest

Bailey, L. H. *How Plants Get Their Names*. New York: Dover, 1963.

Bailey, Liberty Hyde, and Ethel Zoe Bailey (eds.). *Hortus Third: a Concise Dictionary of Plants Cultivated in the United States and Canada*. New York: Macmillan, 1976.

Bailey, Ralph (ed.). *The Good Housekeeping Illustrated Encyclopedia of Gardening* (16 vols.). New York: Hearst, 1972.

Barton, Barbara J. *Gardening by Mail*. San Francisco: Tusker Press, 1986.

Borror, Donald J., and Richard E. White. *A Field Guide to the Insects of America North of Mexico*. Boston: Houghton Mifflin, 1970.

Britton, Nathaniel Lord, and Hon. Addison Brown. *An Illustrated Flora of the Northern United States and Canada* (3 vols.). New York: Dover, 1970.

Brown, Lauren. *Grasses: An Identification Guide*. Boston: Houghton Mifflin, 1979.

Bush-Brown, James, and Louise Bush-Brown. *America's Garden Book*. New York: Charles Scribner's Sons, 1967.

Coombes, Allen J. *Dictionary of Plant Names*. Portland, Ore.: Timber Press, 1985.

Cowell, F. R. *The Garden as a Fine Art*. Boston: Houghton Mifflin, 1978.

Cravens, Richard H. *Pests and Diseases*. Alexandria, Va.: Time-Life, 1977.

Dana, Mrs. William Starr. *How to Know the Wild Flowers*. New York: Dover, 1963.

Dwelley, Marilyn J. *Summer & Fall Wildflowers of New England.* Camden, Me.: Down East Enterprises, 1977.

Friend, Hilderic. *Flower Lore.* Rockport, Mass.: Para Research, 1981.

Haring, Elda. *The Complete Book of Growing Plants from Seed.* New York: Hawthorn Books, 1967.

Harper, Pamela, and Frederick McGourty. *Perennials: How to Select, Grow & Enjoy.* Tucson, Ariz.: HP Books, 1985.

Hayes, Jack (ed.). *Living on a Few Acres, The Yearbook of Agriculture 1978.* Washington, D.C.: U.S. Department of Agriculture, 1978.

Heriteau, Jacqueline. *Grow It and Cook It.* New York: Ballantine, 1970.

Hickey, Michael, and Clive King. *100 Families of Flowering Plants.* London: Cambridge University Press, 1981.

Lloyd, Christopher. *The Well-Chosen Garden.* New York: Harper & Row, 1984.

Loewer, Peter. *Gardens by Design.* Emmaus, Pa.: Rodale, 1986.

Niering, William A., and Nancy C. Olmstead. *The Audubon Society Field Guide to North American Wildflowers, Eastern Region.* New York: Knopf, 1979.

Organic Gardening magazine. *The Encyclopedia of Organic Gardening.* Emmaus, Pa.: Rodale, 1978.

Perry, Frances (ed.). *Simon and Schuster's Complete Guide to Plants and Flowers.* New York: Simon and Schuster, 1974.

Peterson, Roger Tory, and Margaret McKenny. *A Field Guide to Wildflowers of Northeastern and North Central North America.* Boston: Houghton Mifflin, 1968.

Petrides, George A. *A Field Guide to Trees and Shrubs.* Boston: Houghton Mifflin, 1958.

Powell, Claire. *The Meaning of Flowers.* Boulder, Col.: Shambhala, 1979.

Rickett, Harold William. *Botany for Gardeners.* New York: Macmillan, 1957.

Riotte, Louise. *Carrots Love Tomatoes.* Charlotte, Vt.: Garden Way, 1975.

Schenk, George. *The Complete Shade Gardener.* Boston: Houghton Mifflin, 1984.

Stearn, William T. *Botanical Latin.* North Pomfret, Vt.: David & Charles, 1986.

Stone, Doris M. *The Great Public Gardens of the Eastern United States.* New York: Pantheon, 1982.

Sugden, Andrew. *Longman Illustrated Dictionary of Botany.* Burnt Mill, Harlow, Essex: Longman York Press, 1984.

U.S. Department of Agriculture. *Complete Guide to Home Canning, Preserving, and Freezing.* New York: Dover, 1973.

Westcott, Cynthia. *The Gardener's Bug Book.* New York: Doubleday, 1973.

White, Katherine S. *Onward and Upward in the Garden.* New York: Farrar, Straus & Giroux, 1981.

Books on Herbs

Boxer, Arabella, and Philippa Back. *The Herb Book.* London: Octopus/Mayflower, 1982.

Boxer, Arabella; Jocasta Innes; Charlotte Parry Crooke; and Lewis Esson. *The Encyclopedia of Herbs, Spices and Flavourings.* New York: Crescent, 1984.

Bunney, Sarah (ed.). *The Illustrated Book of Herbs.* New York: Gallery Books, 1984.

Clarkson, Rosetta E. *The Golden Age of Herbs & Herbalists.* New York: Dover, 1972.

Coon, Nelson. *Using Plants for Healing.* Emmaus, Pa.: Rodale, 1979.

———. *Using Wild and Wayside Plants.* New York: Dover, 1980.

Crockett, James Underwood, and Ogden Tanner. *Herbs.* Alexandria, Va.: Time-Life, 1977.

Edinger, Philip (ed.). *How to Grow Herbs.* Menlo Park, Calif.: Lane Books, 1972.

Fielder, Mildred. *Fielder's Herbal Helper for Hunters, Trappers, and Fishermen.* Tulsa, Okla.: Winchester Press, 1982.

Foley, Daniel J. (ed.). *Herbs for Use and for Delight. An Anthology* from *The Herbarist*, a publication of the Herb Society of America. New York: Dover, 1974.

Foster, Gertrude B. *Herbs for Every Garden*. New York: E. P. Dutton, 1973.

Foster, Gertrude B., and Rosemary F. Louden. *Park's Success with Herbs*. Greenwood, S.C.: Geo. W. Park Seed Co., 1980.

Fox, Helen Morgenthau. *Gardening with Herbs for Flavor and Fragrance*. New York: Dover, 1970.

Gerard, John. *The Herbal or General History of Plants*. New York: Dover, 1975.

Gordon, Lesley. *A Country Herbal*. New York: Gallery Books, 1984.

Grieve, M. *Culinary Herbs & Condiments*. New York: Dover, 1971.

———. *A Modern Herbal* (2 vols.). New York: Dover, 1971.

Hayes, Elizabeth S. *Spices and Herbs: Lore and Cookery*. New York: Dover, 1980.

Hylton, William H. (ed.). *The Rodale Herb Book*. Emmaus, Pa.: Rodale, 1979.

Kamm, Minnie Watson. *Old Time Herbs for Northern Gardens*. New York: Dover, 1971.

Lathrop, Norma Jean. *Herbs: How to Select, Grow and Enjoy*. Tucson, Ariz.: H. P. Books, 1981.

Mazza, Irma Goodrich. *Herbs for the Kitchen*. Boston: Little, Brown, 1976.

Millspaugh, Charles F. *American Medicinal Plants*. New York: Dover, 1974.

Potter, David (ed.). *Culpeper's Color Herbal*. New York: Sterling, 1983.

Rohde, Eleanour S. *A Garden of Herbs*. New York: Dover, 1969.

Shaudys, Phyllis. *The Pleasure of Herbs*. Pownal, Vt.: Garden Way, 1986.

Stuart, Malcolm (ed.). *VNR Color Dictionary of Herbs & Herbalism*. New York: Van Nostrand Reinhold, 1982.

Tolley, Emilie, and Chris Mead. *Herbs: Gardens, Decorations, and Food*. New York: Crown, 1985.

Weiner, Michael A. *Earth Medicine — Earth Foods.* New York: Macmillan, 1972.

Books on Everlastings

Carico, Nita Cox, and Jane Calvert Guynn. *The Dried-Flower Book.* New York: Doubleday, 1962.

Cormack, Alan, and David Carter. *Flowers: Growing, Drying, Preserving.* New York: Crescent, 1987.

Embertson, Jane. *Pods, Wildflowers and Weeds in Their Final Beauty.* New York: Charles Scribner's Sons, 1979.

Hillier, Malcolm, and Colin Hilton. *The Book of Dried Flowers.* New York: Simon and Schuster, 1986.

Mierhof, Annette. *The Dried Flower Book.* New York: E. P. Dutton, 1981.

Silber, Mark, and Terry Silber. *The Book of Everlastings: Growing, Drying and Designing with Dried Flowers.* New York: Knopf, 1988.

Squires, Mabel. *The Art of Drying Plants & Flowers.* New York: Bonanza Books, 1958.

Thorpe, Patricia. *Everlastings: The Complete Book of Dried Flowers.* Boston: Houghton Mifflin, 1986.

Wiita, Betty. *Dried Flowers for All Seasons.* New York: Van Nostrand Reinhold, 1982.

DATE DUE